P

CHRIST A

MW00807150

"In nearly 50 pieces, ranging from short paragraphs to lengthy essays Gram provides readers with inspirational notes....Written just prior to George Floyd's death, which Gram laments in his introduction, his daily musings sometimes discuss racism, particularly anti-Asian violence and rhetoric. A final essay concludes with the author's vivid story of overcoming a genetic blood-clotting disorder. After the diagnosis he became a prolific mountain climber and rode his bicycle from California to New Hampshire at the age of 68...Though the author is a mainline Protestant, he intentionally includes other faith traditions in his remarks, from Roman Catholicism to Buddhism...Gram's lucid writing style is that of a seasoned and intellectual yet nurturing pastor...An uplifting, relevant devotional for finding hope in darkness."
—*Kirkus Reviews*

"His prayers are one of the truest treasures of the book. While many written prayers can come across as overly formal, stilted and stuffy, Gram's are refreshingly short, honest, and natural expressions of the emotions faced in the middle of challenge." —Jessica Tofino Educator and Writer 5 Stars

"You write beautifully—the language flows, the references and allusions are apt; you skillfully apply scripture to treat the psychological and spiritual wounds inflicted by the covid pandemic—the fear confusion and loneliness of those you address. I was particularly taken by the evocative writing and arresting figuration of your final meditation. The account of your mountain ascent is a wonderful piece of descriptive writing. I could almost feel the piercing cold, the muscle cramps, the panic of your fall!" —Rev. Dr. Paul R. Fries Ph.D., Emeritus Professor of Foundational and Constructive Theology, New Brunswick Theological Seminary

"I was more than pleasantly surprised by the casual and intense wisdom dispensed in little penny packets that can be taken when the need arises. Thanks Doc!" —Brad Butler, Author

"These meditations are both timely and timeless and bespeak the fact that the pastor not only speaks to those he serves, but listens to them. Now we can listen and learn from these theologically vibrant, psychologically sound and winsomely written offerings." —Rev. Norman Kolenbrander, Reformed Church in America pastor

"These observations are not confined to the dusty or cliched biblical past. Rev. Gram addresses the issue of the discrimination he sees in the pandemic...There's something in this book for everyone regardless of political or religious persuasion. As Rev. Gram says. 'This book is not meant to convert but to console.' It is also a book that will make you remember that we have been tested many times before as evidenced by the many biblical analogies and lessons in the book."—Jim Langan, Editor, *The Hudson Valley News*

"You offer the world something which relieves suffering...*Christ and Covid-19* will still be valuable once we get back to normal life. This offering helps regardless of the struggle people are going through. Even the cover of your book is so peaceful." —Kimberly Love. 'Crashing 40', Impact Radio USA

"The book shows a real and hopeful look at how Christ and prayer must be part of the wonders it can bring to help the pandemic, this book brings that hope for those to understand that Christ can still be the answer." —Ron Specker-Program Director, KLTF Radio Little Falls MN

"Rev. Gram has great insight and wisdom. His book guides us through difficult times by centering our thoughts and cultivating hope." —Ron Van Dam, New England Broadcasting

CHRIST *and* COVID-19

MEDITATIONS FOR PEACE IN TIMES OF TURMOIL

Rev. Dr. Robert L. Gram

Epigraph Books

Rhinebeck, New York

Paperback ISBN 978-1-951937-44-7
eBook ISBN 978-1-951937-45-4

Library of Congress Control Number 2020910944

Book design by Colin Rolfe
Cover art by Bardet Wardell
Back cover photo: Huayna Potosi

Epigraph Books
22 East Market Street, Suite 304
Rhinebeck, NY 12572
(845) 876-4861
epigraphps.com

To Sarah, Joanna, and Lily, my daughters
Elyse, Joanna, Beckett, and Bryton, my grandchildren.

To the victims of coronavirus, and those who mourn their passing.

"Even in our sleep, pain which cannot forget falls
drop by drop upon the heart
Until, in our own despair, against our will,
comes wisdom through the awful grace of God."

Aeschylus

"I am the resurrection and the life"

Jesus

INTRODUCTION

I wrote the following for parishioners and friends of St. John's Reformed Church in Red Hook, New York. The church hired me as interim pastor last October when their full time minister underwent serious surgery, entailing several months of recuperation. The pastor's medical complications prolonged my tenure which should have ended in March. Covid-19 exploded in our area by then. We suspended worship in the sanctuary, and I started preaching on YouTube. Because of the virus, pastors couldn't perform tasks like home and hospital visitation. I felt the need to do more in light of this sudden and startling tragedy. Thus the writing of meditations compensated for the pastoral roles Covid-19 had stolen.

I retired from full time ministry in 2017. Some pastors end their careers publishing sermons, prayers, or meditations. When I left the parish I overslept for the first three months, catching up for the gradual depletion most clerics experience after decades of service. Fully awake, I still believed I had nothing to write which would interest me, let alone a passing reader. This still may be the case. But Covid-19 provided a challenge, like an onrushing train, which couldn't be ignored. In the wake of the terror, a hope dispensing Jesus needed proclamation.

The poet T.S. Eliot wrote: "And so each venture is a new beginning, a raid on the inarticulate/With shabby equipment always deteriorating/In the general mess of imprecision of feeling, Undisciplined squads of emotion" (Four Quartets). That pretty much sums up my writing. I'm not indulging in false modesty. Its simply hard for words to capture the present threat. And perhaps my devotionals have a personal element which deprives of wider application. Covid-19 infiltrates not only because friends and valued colleagues have died. I am predisposed, a high risk in the coronavirus hierarchy. Maybe the preacher is preaching to his, at times, fear ridden self.

The meditations are divided by the church seasons: In the

mid-Hudson Valley, Covid-19 spread during Lent. For Christians Lent is a period of penitence, and self examination. It is often marked by ascetic practices such as fasting. Lent yields to Holy Week. It begins with Jesus' triumphal entry into Jerusalem, Palm Sunday, and ends with his death. The meditations for Holy Week focus primarily on Jesus' dying words from the cross. Easter follows, and the church turns to resurrection. I end with the feast of Pentecost where the Holy Spirit insufflates the disciples with foreign languages, they could not have learned on their own. Living mindfully within church seasons orders life. This is important now that Covid-19 has destroyed our calendrical sense. Sports played in Spring are postponed to Winter. Traditional entertainments on beaches and outdoor arenas have been cancelled. Schools may or may not open in September. Our usual time markers skew.

My use of the church calendar does not abide by lectionary readings—specific Scriptural texts for specific days—which greater church bodies assign. The meditations were driven by the exigencies of parishioner mood, and the nightly news. It may appear as if Lent, Holy Week, Easter, and Pentecost are merely segmental breaks, convenient denotations without the lectionary heft the seasons deserve. That's true.

The narratives lack uniform length. I wrote shorter meditations initially as you will see. The first three are abbreviated particularly; perhaps I was dipping my toes before taking the plunge. At the end of the book, the last entry expands beyond my working definition of 'meditation'; it counterbalances shorter pieces. The last narrative is also different in kind. It concerns a mountain climbing incident, seventeen years earlier, whose parabolic implications were realized in a dream shortly before Pentecost Sunday.

The meditations have been edited. Some pieces are longer than first written. I have not, however, retrojected later events into earlier material. This is important in one instance. One cannot write about disease in general without mentioning discrimination. Throughout history epidemics and racism go in hand. I describe a few examples. I wrote before the death of Mr. Floyd. I have let the meditations stand as they are rather than adding insight from the Minneapolis tragedy. Thus the book rests on daily comings and goings, unalloyed by future events.

I am a Christian, but pray this book helps people of all faiths, or no faith. It is not meant to convert, but to console. And provide hope. Some meditations are taken from the Hebrew Scripture, a joy to read. Others have been influenced by Buddhist thought. My doctoral work centered on the great medieval Christian mystic, Meister Eckhart, regarded rightly as a bodhisattva by my Buddhist brothers and sisters. Studying other religions facilitates greater understanding of one's own. At least that's my experience. Nevertheless some familiarity with Christianity helps. I did not write for a general audience, but rather a small congregation wrestling with the theological implications of this pandemic. I hope something here aids your pilgrimage, whatever lodestar guides.

Thanks to Rev. James and Joan Alley for suggesting a book format. Thanks to Shari Juranic, St. John's Church administrator, for compiling, and gently keeping me to a deadline. I am indebted to the parishioners of St. John's who serve the needs of their community in truly Christ-like ways. They are an amazing group. Thanks to George Rodenhausen and Bardet Wardell, my dear friends. And to Ernest Shaw, my pillar. Finally I am beholden to Colin Rolfe, and the dedicated staff at Epigraph.

LENT

1
_____

SCRIPTURE:

"Dear children, let us love not in words or speech, but with actions and truth" 1st John 3:18.

Walking around my condo complex, I passed a woman who crossed to the other side as I neared. "It's not you," she said. "It's social distancing. I hope you're not offended." On the contrary. Her movement was kindness toward me and precaution for her. Loving acts are grander, we think—a special dinner at a great restaurant; a prized gift, a romantic getaway. During the pandemic, loving may involve something much simpler: Giving someone literal space so that he or she may not contract what we may or may not have. Such acts are the sinew and bone of compassion.

PRAYER:

Lord, let me be an instrument of your love. Use me as you see fit. Grace me with a cautious spirit in my inter-actions. Let me understand that faith shines through social distancing. In the name of my healing Savior, I pray. Amen.

2

———

> "Jesus knew that the Father had put all things under
> his power, and that he had come from God and was
> returning to God; so he got up from the meal, took off
> his outer clothing, and wrapped around his waist. After
> that he poured water into a basin and began to wash
> his disciples' feet, drying them with a towel that was
> wrapped around him" John 13:3-5.

Jesus' loving act occurs after celebrating his last supper in Jerusalem before his betrayal, trial and execution. The author of the Fourth Gospel is not particularly interested in the words of institution employed by the other three Gospel writers—the instruction before, during and after the Lord's Supper, when bread and wine come to symbolize Jesus' broken body and spilled blood. It seems the sacrament for John is foot washing itself, which he describes carefully. He invites one to explore its implication. In light of the pandemic, I'm not suggesting that we wash others' feet; but it's a great idea to wash our own! And our hands, too.

Perhaps God calls us to turn foot and hand washing into sacramental acts. In the latter, we discover calm by focusing on the warmth of the water, the soap as it foams; and noting, as we rinse, the amazing grasping, and digital abilities of the 'gadgets' at arms' end. Let's go further. Suppose we are invited to sacralize all basics of daily living? Doing so involves slowing our pace. One cannot read this text, and believe that Jesus hurried through foot washing. John's narrative prevents a quick moving on. So one imagines Jesus scrubbing between his disciples' toes, liberating dirt, nearly impacted by the demands of itinerancy. When drying, God's son kneads arches, and heels briskly until stress, which feet carry, releases.

Let coronavirus goad us to spot the sacred in the dailiness of life. Social isolation may provide greater opportunity. Every morning it's breakfast before church work. I start with orange juice. Today I noted the sensory process after that first sip, how sweet tendrils spread from my mouth to the hinge of my jaw. Pay attention to the course of that tang—whatever fruit juice you favor—or the aroma of brewing coffee as you begin your life anew each morning. The Psalmist writes, "O taste and see that the Lord is good!"(34:8). Indeed. What other miracles await you this hour, this moment?

PRAYER:

> Lord, help me experience the abundance each day
> offers by discovering blessings disguised. May I delight
> in what I touch, see, smell, and taste. Slow me so that I
> sense your presence whatever I do. In the name of my
> healing Savior, I pray. Amen.

3

SCRIPTURE:

"I sought the Lord and he answered me; he delivered me from all my fears" Psalm 34:9.

The coronavirus scares, often beyond our imagining. The theologian, Paul Tillich, once wrote that fear is our primal emotion. I'm no authority, but I've read that some, if not most, anthropologists support this view, speculating that we are hardwired because our slow ancestors provided dinner for faster carnivores. Thus the Neanderthal could anticipate and escape the leopard prowling in the distance because terror motivated and mobilized his resources. In our Covid-19 context, fear, and its adrenaline rush, may speed safety measures for ourselves, and those in need. Harnessed anxiety aids.

The Bible alludes to fear unchecked, however, which overwhelms our rational and coping capacities. That's understandable. Our Neanderthal could at least spot the leopard. How do we outwit a predator who carries off its victims in an invisible maw?

The Psalmist states that God has saved him already from 'fears'— note the past tense and plural. Can we still anxiety, by remembering God's fright wresting ability throughout our lives? A character in a short story by Charles Dickens prays, "Oh, Lord, keep my memory green." During the pandemic, may we faithfully recollect our history. Our deliverance in the past will surely continue in the present.

PRAYER:

Lord, help me to rely more fully on your love, and care. You know me better than I know myself. You love me more than I love myself. Deliver me from the marauder's terror, that I may serve you more faithfully. In the name of our healing Savior, I pray. Amen.

4

SCRIPTURE:

"God says, 'Be still and know that I am God'" Psalm 46:10.

Is it harder to be still outside or if we are in quarantine? My sense is that restlessness pervades more when we are in lock-down mode. It may manifest itself in pacing back and forth, or walking from one floor to another without a clue of what motivated us to do so. In the book of Job, Satan defines himself as one "roaming throughout the earth, going back and forth on it." The 20th Century Trappist monk, Thomas Merton, once noted that the Devil's middle name is "Busyness." The anxiety which the pandemic stokes is purposeless energy, a fidgety activity which may be as contagious to loved ones as the virus itself. And restlessness can be manifest even when we're immobile. We all know how anxiety causes our minds, if not our bodies, to race. The Buddhists refer to this state as "Monkey Mind". Thoughts flit in and out faster than a hummingbird wing. God calls us to know him by being still physically and mentally.

Throughout Christian history, monks have practiced stilling themselves and focusing on God. How might we do that? Breathing deeply is a start. Feel the lungs pulling air in, and then releasing. Focusing on breath alone will bring us where we need to be. Sit in a straight backed chair. Think of nothing but God filling Adam's lungs for the first time. Sense your Creator in the ebb and flow of respiration. Every breath bespeaks of God's continual presence in each moment of our lives. What new perceptions about the wonder of reality will you gather as you pay attention to your breath? The great short story writer, Franz Kafka, once penned: "You do not have to leave your room. Remain sitting at your table and listen. Do not even listen. Simply wait. Do not even wait. Be quite still, and solitary. The world will freely offer itself to you, to be unmasked. It will roll in ecstasy at your feet."

PRAYER:

> Loving Father, remove restlessness from my being.
> Still the fear which drives unnecessary movement.
> May I remember your presence in every breath I take.
> Without saying a word, may the peace you bestow on
> your servant bring calm and repose to those around me.
> In the name of our healing Savior I pray. Amen.

5

SCRIPTURE:

> "When Jesus had entered Capernaum, a centurion came
> to him, asking for help. 'Lord,' he said. 'My servant
> lies at home paralyzed, suffering terribly.' Jesus said
> to him, 'Shall I come and heal him?' The centurion
> replied, 'Lord I do not deserve to have you come under
> my roof. But just say the word, and my servant will be
> healed. For I myself am a man under authority, with
> soldiers under me. I tell this one 'Go', and he goes, and
> that one , 'Come', and he comes. I say this to my ser-
> vant, 'Do this,' and he does it." When Jesus heard this,
> he was amazed and said to those following him, 'Truly
> I tell you, I have not found anyone in Israel with such
> great faith'" Matthew 8:5-11.

This story is important for us during this pandemic for two reasons.
First, we understand that the centurion's faith is valued because he
executes authority. As a Roman commander of 100 soldiers, he saw
that Jesus, too, possessed executive ability so that his orders would
be implemented from a distance. I believe that God calls us to exercise loving control over others, much like the faithful captain.

Your family, particularly your children, may be looking for you
to make the hard decision, the difficult call: 'Why can't I play with
my friends in the play room? How about the back yard?' 'What time
should I go to the supermarket?' Mom/Dad, I really want restaurant take-out. Uncle Ted works there and says it's safe.' 'My friends
are gathering in downtown Red Hook. They'll be 7 of us. That's a
little less than 10. I'll be safe.' 'I know my boyfriend/girlfriend has
no symptoms. And he/she works out everyday. Why can't we hold
hands? Why can't we kiss.'. Exercising authority becomes more

difficult when God is thrown into the mix. Suddenly we are forced to be theologians: Mom/Dad you say that God loves and protects us. If that's the case why do I have to follow man-made rules?' 'Look, I'm young, healthy, and all of my friends are going to Florida on their Spring break. If you really have faith in God, you'll let me go.' The 'authority ante' is upped, too, when we are called to make decisions regarding adults: 'Why can't you visit? I'm told they clean everything in this nursing home/senior center.'

Exercising authority can be profoundly difficult. But God calls each of us to take charge even when we believe that leadership is the least of our gifts. Both Moses and Jeremiah felt that way. There are many terrified individuals who need our authority exercising ability. God will equip us if we say 'Yes' to his call. And He will reveal gifts we never thought we possessed. Ironically the virus may produce in us a surge of self-confidence.

The second point is that Jesus exercised authority from a distance. He healed the centurion's servant, although our Lord may have been miles away. In this brave new world of social distancing, we are called to make decisions over the phone or computer. If we believe in what God would have us do, we'll have the passion to make our wills known, even from afar.

PRAYER:

> Lord often I lack the confidence to exercise leadership.
> Sometimes I'm afraid to say 'No' to people I love.
> Often I believe that the word 'authority' and all it con-
> notes runs against the grain of my spirit. Lord, use me
> as you will. Through this panicky period, may my calm
> presence, and wise words still the fears of many. I pray
> in the name of our healing Savior. Amen.

6

SCRIPTURE:

> "This is what the Lord Almighty, the God of Israel,
> says to all those I carried into exile from Jerusalem to
> Babylon: Build houses and settle down; plant gardens
> and eat what they produce. Marry and have sons and
> daughters; find wives for your sons, and give your
> daughters in marriage, so they, too, may have sons
> and daughters...Do not let the prophets and diviners
> among you deceive you. Do not listen to the dreams
> you encourage them to have" Jeremiah 294-6, 8.

Some pundits believe the virus will end in July or August. Others are more optimistic. Covid-19 will not go past Easter Sunday which we celebrate soon. I don't buy either assessment. We may have to hunker down and prepare for a longer stretch. In our text, the prophet Jeremiah sends a letter to his fellow Jews who have been exiled in Babylon. Jerusalem had been sacked in 586 B.C. by Nebuchadnezzar, and much of the intelligentsia were marched off in chains, hundreds of miles to the east in what is now Iraq. The exiles believed God would reverse their fortunes quickly. And they spawned prophets and soothsayers to communicate exactly what they wanted to hear.

God's letter dashes their hopes. They're not returning the day after tomorrow. The Almighty tells them to settle in their new surroundings, and essentially bloom where they do not want to be planted. Embrace life in the present, although you reside in enemy territory. Eat, drink, marry and have children. Do not grieve the past. That's good advice for us, who long for a speedy return to the way things were before Covid-19's captivity.

What does it mean for us to live fully in the present? We may discover new ways to experience hope, and joy. I have a hunch.

We won't be as busy. We may have more time for family, and less time running here, there, and everywhere. There may be increased moments for walking outdoors rather than sprinting through corridors. There will be time to post a handwritten letter, and less time to dash off post-it notes.

What new avenues will lead to fulfillment? The disease forces us to ask. Be patient, God tells us. The pandemic will end. In 539 B.C., a coalition of Medes and Persians destroyed the Babylonian empire, and Jews were allowed to return to their homeland. Captivity did not last forever. Neither will ours.

PRAYER:

> Lord, help me to find meaning in this new world. Give me patience. Grant me the ability to see where joy and hope might be hidden. Help me to thrive in coronavirus captivity. Let me liberate those ensnared by nostalgia. In the name of my healing Savior, I pray. Amen.

7

> "An angel carried me away in the Spirit to a moun-
> tain great and high, and showed me the Holy City,
> Jerusalem, coming down out of heaven from God. It
> shone with the glory of God, and its brilliance was like
> that of a very precious jewel, like jasper, clear as crys-
> tal...The wall was made of jasper, and the city of pure
> gold, as pure as glass. The foundations of the city walls
> were decorated with every kind of precious stone. The
> first foundation was jasper, the second sapphire, the
> third agate, the fourth emerald...The twelve gates of
> the city were twelve pearls, each gate made of a single
> pearl. The great street of the city was of gold, as pure
> as transparent glass" Revelation 21: 10-11; 19-21.

The author of the last book of the Bible, John, surpassed our condition in terms of social isolation. He authored Revelation while
in exile on the island of Patmos. This rocky outcrop lies 50 miles
southwest of the ancient city of Ephesus, in what is now Turkey, By
the time of Roman Emperor Domitian (81-96 A.D.), it was used as
a Roman penal colony. Prisoners there remanded were often placed
in open air isolation. That seems to be the case for the writer of
Revelation. In spite of his isolation, or because of it, John wrote
concerning the ultimate triumph of good over evil.

Near the end of his work he described the heavenly Jerusalem
which would descend, establishing a new heaven and earth-- the
climactic end of human history. Because he had no access to modern media, he does his best, piling on gem stone colors, creating
a mind-popping glimpse of the future for his contemporaries. The
novelist Herman Melville, among others, noted that God is found

in the details. Throughout his book, the Revelator seems to share Melville's view. Phantasmagoric images as well as colors crowd his narrative. It's a descriptive masterpiece.

In our housebound state, I believe God will grant us hopeful visions of a nearing future once the pandemic ends, which it will. God calls us to imagine what we will be doing, what we will be thinking, and who we will be hugging, and kissing, What restaurants will we frequent again? What cinemas, and theaters will we attend? Is a weekend trip to NYC in your future? Whenever I pass the Starr Library in Rhinebeck, it whispers, "I miss you Uncle Bob." "I miss you too," I respond. "Someday our love-fest will continue," I assure it. And it will. The more detail we insert into our dreams and imaginings, the more hopeful our lives will become.

PRAYER:

> Great God still my anxious heart. Whenever fear arises, implant a hopeful vision in my being. Let me ride out this pandemic on the wings of your never ending love. Help me to envision a time in which I revel in the joys of the life you have called me to live, unshackled from disease and its terrors. I pray in the name of my healing Savior, Jesus. Amen.

8

> "Now on his way to Jerusalem, Jesus traveled along
> the border between Samaria and Galilee. As he was
> going into a village, ten men who had leprosy met him.
> They stood at a distance, and called out in a loud voice,
> 'Jesus, Master, have pity on us!' When he saw them he
> said, 'Go show yourselves to the priests. And as they
> went, they were cleansed. One of them, when he saw
> that he was healed, came back, praising God in a loud
> voice. He threw himself at Jesus' feet and thanked
> him—and he was a Samaritan. Jesus asked, 'Were not
> all ten cleansed? Where are the other nine? Has no one
> returned to give praise to God except this foreigner?'
> Then he said to him, 'Rise and go; your faith has made
> you well'" Luke 17:11-19.

Usually the Lord's work is one-on-one. Here Jesus attends to 10 very
sick people at once. Today health professionals have or will experience convergent sick at hospital entrances and emergency rooms.
Leprosy can be equated with Covid-19. In Jesus' day leprosy was
incurable and widespread. Those afflicted were quarantined in col-
onies, far from the healthy. If a leper entered a village, he or she
would ring a bell, so villagers could run the other way, or chase the
unfortunate beyond the outskirts. We may be missing the clang, but
friends mention those returning home from hospitals who face, if
not threat, then subtle discrimination. Social distancing exponen-
tializes as the recovering languish in spatial wildernesses.

I am grateful to all our health workers who confront an intrac-
table illness which has yet no cure. Just as Jesus confronted leprosy.
Their bravery inverts social distancing. Hands-on work which may

come at a costly price. The above text is anomalous because Jesus often healed by physical contact—raising the ill and dead with a yank; placing mud on a blind man's eyes. He literally touched the untouchable. Just like physicians and nurses today.

Three aspects of our text are particularly interesting. First, cure comes from a stranger, a 'foreigner', as Jesus states. Today patients express profound gratitude for the nurses and physicians who reassure, and comfort. The healer's race and ethnicity matter little when survival is at stake. My hope is that Covid-19 mortally wounds discrimination. Let's imagine a black or brown arm cradling a Caucasian head, a noggin prejudice filled, until such loving concern banishes racist leanings as quickly as Christ liberated the demon possessed.

The health care worker may be 'adopted' by a grateful patient, and the family. The physician and nurse may discover they are kin now. In light of healing, how many invidious distinctions will vanish? Many I hope. The author of the book of Hebrews writes: "Do not neglect to show hospitality to strangers. For by doing that, some have entertained angels unaware" (Hebrews 13:2). Even from a distance one may catch the multicolored wing batting in hospitals, nursing homes, and assisted living facilities!

Second, Jesus presents at the right time. His miracle working fame may have preceded, but who knew he'd walk by the Samaritan boarder just when the ten needed him most? This is one example of many underpinning Scripture's take on reality: The world is providential rather than coincidental. Jesus always shows up the very moment he can do the most good. So do our front line workers. And, if we move beyond the parameters of pandemic, so do we.

At midnight on Juy 1st, 1997, Hong Kong was ceded to mainland China. Near that date my former wife and I adopted our Chinese daughter, Lily. Several days before we met her, I asked our guide if we could stop at a church on the way to the adoption center in the city of Changsha. It was Sunday. Our guide discovered one, but noted that many had been turned into indoctrination centers. Such was the case here. The cross and steeple had been removed, and the former cinder block sanctuary, now disused, radiated must, and abandonment indicating, positively, that people had better things to do than listen to Chairman Mao's Little Red Book quoted from the pulpit.

We stopped at a visitors' center beside the church. An old woman greeted us. When I told her my occupation in the smidge of Mandarin I knew, she scurried to another room and introduced a woman in her early 20's who had been packing for return to her hometown. The elderly woman explained to our guide that her young friend had become a Christian two years earlier. She despaired because she wanted a "real minister" to baptize her. Would that ever happen, the girl wondered? Well, it happened that day.

Finally only one in ten expresses gratitude to Jesus. In light of this pandemic, thankfulness is essential. Let it percolate through your being. The more facets of life gratitude embraces, the happier and healthier we will be. It begins with expressions to those who have been our physicians spiritually as well as physically. In enjoining the ten to meet a priest, Jesus represents both. Let me go futher. Gratitude blossoms when it grasps realities beyond sentience.

Along with a part time pastorate, I worked as an outpatient substance abuse clinician in Manhattan for four years. One evening a client arrived drenched from a sudden thunderstorm. He was a man in his late 30's, and had been alcohol dependent since his early teens. He was always optimistic, but this day ecstasy greeted me. I asked about the change. "Well, I was standing on a street corner, and I found myself staring at a puddle," he said. "I noticed the color of the oil in the water, mostly blue swirls. I kept looking until I realized I'd be late coming here." I asked him what he felt, standing there. "Thankfulness", he said. The event was linchpin toward his eventual abstinence. Gratitude for a miniature oil slick!

Let thankfulness ramify to such a degree that poet William Blake's words become yours: "To see a World in a Grain of Sand/ And a Heaven in a Wild Flower, Hold Infinity in the palm of your hand/ And eternity in an hour."

PRAYER:

God, I thank you for creating so many people who sacrifice personal safety in order to help the sick and vulnerable. May they sense my prayers for them as well as the patients they treat. Guide their skillful hands, through the power of your Spirit, and give them hope that their efforts will yield cure. I pray in the name of our healing Savior Jesus Christ. Amen.

9

SCRIPTURE:

> "Wearing a linen ephod, David was dancing before the
> Lord with all his might, while he and all Israel were
> bringing up the ark of the Lord with shouts, and the
> sound of trumpets. As the ark of the Lord was entering
> the City of David, Michal daughter of Saul watched
> from a window... she saw King David leaping and
> dancing before the Lord" 2 Samuel 6:14-16.

Anthropologists believe that an early art form, if not the earliest,
is dance. I've seen my daughters move to musical beats shortly
after leaving their crawl. The Bantus of South Africa will not ask
a stranger, 'What is your name?', but, 'How do you dance?' The
Chinese philosopher, Confucius, once stated, 'I understand a people
by the way they dance.' John Gleeson writes about his return from
the Viet Nam War, noting how his arthritic grandmother, whose
posture resembled a question mark, cast her walker aside, and performed an Irish jig to express her joy.

Would dancing remove the homebound isolation you feel? Would
it diminish fear of infection? Would it mitigate mourning for lost
jobs, and dwindling retirement accounts? It might. In the above text,
King David dances for joy. The presence of God in the ark of the
covenant has been carried to his new capital, Jerusalem. In Jesus'
famous parable, the Father embraces the Prodigal Son, and then
celebrates his return by feasting, and dancing (Luke 15:25). Any
sort of activity which gets hearts pumping, and bodies moving abets
spiritual vitality, especially if, like King David, we do it with all our
might.

Dancing, among other forms of exercise, gets us out of our head.
It's a 'no brainer'! Our bodies commandeer our minds as we focus

on movement. Before Covid-19, I instructed indoor cycling. Between taxing routines, the group would rest by pace slowing. We eased, but never stopped peddling. It is during such breaks that legs often maintain a higher cadence than the mind signals. 'Slow down', the brain commands. 'Not as much as you'd like', the quads reply. At times our bodies desire independence from our anxiety producing gray matter, especially during the pandemic.

What if you can't dance, run, or walk? God will empower you to perform something which engages your body. Early in my ministry I met a wheel chair bound woman in her late-80's. Her daily routine involved bicep curls with light barbells, followed by 'tap dancing', as she put it, in which her fingers pattered across a desk. "I'm a regular Fred Astaire", she laughed. My parishioner believed her effort honored God. Most certainly it did.

PRAYER:

Great God, let me counter mourning with dancing. And may it be done for your glory. In the name of our healing Savior I pray. Amen.

10

SCRIPTURE:

> "Praise be to the God and Father of our Lord Jesus
> Christ, the Father of compassion, and the God of all
> comfort who comforts us all in our troubles, so that
> we can comfort those in any trouble with the comfort
> we ourselves receive" 2 Corinthians 1:3-4.

> "Then people brought little children to Jesus for him
> to place his hands on them and pray for them. But
> the disciples rebuked them. Jesus said, 'Let the little
> children come to me, and do not hinder them, for the
> kingdom of heaven belongs to such as these'" Matthew
> 19:13-14.

Jesus states that we must become like children to enter God's kingdom. What might that mean? Commonly we believe we should strive for a child's faith, joy, and spontaneity. That's true. Jesus may have had something additional in mind.

First, children understand very clearly what they need from adults. They're not shy about asking. And they won't take no for an answer. They understood Jesus had something to offer even if his 'party-pooper' disciples believed their master had better things to do than bless children.

Several years ago my adopted daughter, Lily, and I flew to California for a reunion with couples who had adopted their Chinese daughters the same day at the social services center in Changsha. After a wonderful celebration hosted by Paul and his wife Tricia, Paul took Lily and I to meet his next door neighbor, Christine, and her adopted daughter, Amanda. Christine's experience was far different than ours. Years earlier she attended a party thrown by a couple who had recently adopted a daughter. Suddenly a five year old approached Christine, and hugged her leg. Looking up, she said, 'I need a mommy. My mommy doesn't want me.' She was quite insistent. She wouldn't let go of her leg. Christine loved her work, and her free personal time. Having a child was the last thing on her mind. 'What could I do?', Christine laughed when she told her story. When we met, Mom was helping her daughter pack for an away volley ball tournament. I believe Jesus wants us to be as open about our needs as Amanda in particular, and children in general.

Second, children understand the need to be comforted. Little ones keen to cuddling, and cooing. Do we? As grown-ups we may assume that word is inapplicable. We're too mature. We're givers not receivers, at this stage, and our purpose is to comfort children, forgetting the need inheres throughout our lives.

Several years ago I entered a nursing home to visit a parishioner. In the foyer, an elderly woman, face in hands, wept. "Is there anything I can do?" I asked. I was dressed in my clerical collar, and added that I was a clergyman. Would she like prayer? Or a hug? She lifted her face and glowered. "Not from you," she replied. "All I want is to crawl up on my mother's lap and be comforted." At that moment a familiar face appeared. The bustling head nurse said, "Oh, Bertha, I'm so sad when you're sad. Would you like a hug?" She nodded, and smiled, wiping her eyes. I headed down the hall toward my congregant's room as they embraced. Strike one for the pastor!

At the Last Supper in John's Gospel, Jesus tells his disciples that God will send them the "Spirit of truth" (14:17; 15:26). Along with the phrase, Jesus mentions the Greek word 'paraclete' which translates as 'advocate', or 'counselor'. As a boy, my minister told me the word meant 'comforter'. To this day I hold that definition even if it's incorrect. At my age, I need a comforter more than an advocate. When this pandemic ends, I will sit next to Bertha, if she'll allow, and hope that beefy uniformed presence will grant me a hug along with my 'friend'!

No doubt the disciples were terrified on that baffling evening. Shortly after the foot washing, the business of betrayal, and condemnation commenced. A cross awaited the following day. Jesus warned them in advance, but the disciples had trouble with the plan. Now they were tied to their master's demolition. Their bodies knew what was up even as their minds retracted. It's a wonder any of them could drink a goblet of wine without slopping, as hands and hearts jittered. But Jesus taught that his spirit, the Comforter, would console them throughout the long, long night and the stifling day which followed. Because of the Holy Spirit, they survived, grew, and changed the world.

We are heirs of the same promise. Jesus will comfort us during interminable times of fear. Think of your early years. When did solace embrace you? As a child my father would tuck me into bed, and say, "Now you're as snug as a bug in a rug." The words were magic, and caused sleep. My mother read Bible stories which had the same dreamy effect. I was cuddled by words. In our Covid-19 world, speech is all we may have to swaddle distant loved ones.

God wants you to receive divine comfort. Open your hearts to it in prayer. Let the Paraclete enter and warm you. Like children be brave, and admit your need for consolatory words and hugs, or virtual hugs at the very least. And when your fear stills, dispense comfort as the Apostle Paul advises. Others truly need what you yourself have been given.

PRAYER:

> Lord Jesus, I am a child in need of your quiet presence.
> Enter my heart and mind, and replace fear with your
> spirit that I might find my rest in you. In the name of
> our healing Savior I pray. Amen.

11

SCRIPTURE:

> "Then Moses stretched out his hand over the sea, and
> all that night the Lord drove the sea back with a strong
> east wind, and turned it into dry land. The waters were
> divided, and the Israelites went through the sea on dry
> ground, with a wall of water on their right and on their
> left. The Egyptians pursued them, and all Pharaoh's
> horses, and chariots, and horsemen followed them
> into the sea...Then the Lord said to Moses, 'Stretch
> our your hand over the sea so that the waters may flow
> back over the Egyptians, and their chariots and horse-
> men.' Moses stretched out his hand over the sea..."
> Exodus 14:21-23; 26-27.

Like the Israelites, we experience terror. Pharaoh's army is now a virus. The Egyptians pursued their prey toward the east; Covid-19 approaches from the south in New York State. We witness its destructive dash, faster than Pharaoh's sleekest chariot. We, too, stand at a psychological and physical brink. Will God rescue us? Will we be swallowed up? Like you, I cannot guess the invaders' reach. But I do know that God will deliver us, one way or another.

Throughout Scripture God has always rescued his people from hopeless situations. It's what God does best. We fail to account for God's Third Option. Binary creatures to a fault, we envision only two choices: Pharaoh's or the Red Sea's prey. A mortal spear thrust, or water flooding the lungs. Life becomes an 'either-or' proposition, which is daunting, but fine if we accept by faith that a third path often presents as miracle. In God's plan there is always another choice. Thus the parting of the Red Sea. Moses must have stood slack-jawed as water rolled up in blue undulating walls. Who could have anticipated that?

Look at the New Testament. After Jesus' crucifixion there seemed but two alternatives for the disciples: Anoint a corpse, and risk exposure and arrest, or hide somewhere, hoping to escape Roman detection. God gave them a third option which defied comprehension, understandably, although Jesus had spoken of his resurrection earlier, on more than one occasion, before they entered Jerusalem.

The third option may arrive as an insight stab, an idea dream installed. Let's reverse Christ's timeline for a moment to see what I mean. Jesus' earthly dad, Joseph, was engaged to Mary. Two thousand years ago engagement was taken more seriously than it is in our society. If immorality was suspected, the male—it was usually his call, the law slanted against women—had to issue his partner a writ of divorce, which had serious implications. Initially he believed Mary's bulge was the result of an adulterous relationship. Jewish law required one of two options: Divorce her publicly, and his affianced became the target of a stone throwing contest in the village square; or separate quietly, thrusting her into the wilderness, which was also a death sentence. Towns were inimical to Scarlet Women, and bolted their gates. Thus Mary was subject to a quick or slow death. Your choice, Joseph.

But God provided a third alternative. Joseph took Mary as his wife. Forget the jeers, and the Op-ed in the Nazareth Gazette stating that this demon possessed cuckold should himself be stoned. What profound courage borne of faith the earthly father of Jesus displayed. God's nature is Third Option—a sacred trinity. And so often it beggars imagination. May we stand before the pestilential presence with hope that, in a way we cannot comprehend, God will provide victory over Covid-19.

PRAYER:

> Great God, fill me with your Holy Spirit. Let me cling to your divine work in history. Help me to believe that you will continue to destroy enemies which threaten.

Still my anxieties. Help me to calm all those you lead me to encounter. I pray in the name of our healing Savior Jesus Christ. Amen.

12

SCRIPTURE:

"This is what the Lord Almighty says, 'Do not listen to
what the prophets are prophesying to you; they fill you
with false hopes'" Jeremiah 23:15,16.

The White House briefing yesterday turned ominous. Even if preventive measures are followed perfectly, we were told over 100,000 people will die. That number was optimistic according to the medical leaders assembled before television cameras. The mortality rate could more than double. The preeminent Dr. Anthony Fauci arrived at the number of 240,000. During the conference, the President noted that we are at war. Certainly. And a glance at literal armed conflicts allows us to ponder the scope of our present conflict. The combined casualty rate from Korea, Viet Nam, and World War 1 is a little over 208,000. According to White House projections, coronavirus would lag only behind the death counts of World War 2, and the Civil War. And this is if we follow established guidelines. Suppose we don't? Suppose social distancing gives way to beach partying? Then what? The experts bandied figures as high as two million. Imagine that. No we can't, can we? The mind staggers beneath the numerical weight. We are in the fight of our lives.

Some may believe the President and his medical advisors were exaggerating, or lying. A scare tactic conference. I don't think so. I believe they told the truth, as much as medical science understands. And truth telling is crucial for our well being. It's important in Scripture. The 6th(BCE) Century prophet, Jeremiah, warned Jerusalem to avoid prophets, so called, who ignored the impending tragedy about to overwhelm the capital. Even Jeremiah's family, and friends plotted against him because of his negativity. He prophesied that the corrupt, God-denying, business as usual mentalities would crash when the Babylonians arrived, sacking Jerusalem, slaughtering most inhabitants, and sending the shackled prisoners into exile.

In our parlance Jeremiah was 'out of touch'. It would have been better if, like other prophets, he offered cheery, greeting card sentiments. But Jeremiah was God's truth teller. As painful as it was for him—and he expresses anguish throughout the eponymous work—he nevertheless remained faithful. The news yesterday scared. Of course. Once the initial shock abates, however, truth calms and sustains. It allows us to prepare for the future. It ignites critical thinking: What must we do to help others and ourselves? What concrete actions must be taken in order to weather the onslaught? Lies can't help. They prevent us from engaging the viral enemy in the present; they lure us into a rosy state of inaction, or worse, emotional paralysis. The lie calls us to lounge and ponder some fairytale future involving no effort on our part.

We were created by God with an inbuilt lie detector. We can spot the con. The underlying assumption of snake oil prophets is that we are incapable of facing harsh realities. We're too weak. And believing so becomes a self-fulfilling prophecy. Lies disempower. Always. But we are strong. We are brave. We are heroes in God's army.

PRAYER:

> Loving Father, I thank you for the strength you have
> provided throughout my life. Help me to face what
> needs to be faced even when fear intrudes. Grant me
> assurance that I'm following your will. Stay by my side.
> Help me to understand that my courage will lay the
> foundation of your ultimate victory. In the name of our
> healing Savior I pray. Amen.

13

SCRIPTURE:

> "The word of the Lord came to me, saying, 'Before I formed you in the womb I knew you, before you were born, I set you apart; I appointed you a prophet to the nations'" Jeremiah 1:4-5.

> "You deceived me, Lord, and I was deceived; you overpowered me and prevailed. I am ridiculed all day long; everyone mocks me. Whenever I speak, I cry out proclaiming violence and destruction. So the word of God has brought me insult and reproach all day long. But if I say, 'I will not mention his word or speak anymore in his name', his word is in my heart like a fire, a fire shut up in my bones. I am weary of holding it in; indeed, I cannot" Jeremiah 20:7-9.

Yesterday's devotional concerned the 6th Century prophet's mission to speak truth to Jerusalem whose inhabitants had forgotten God. Such forgetfulness led to idol worship. Its practical application often involved infant sacrifice on the altars of foreign gods' dotting the hills around the city. In Jeremiah's day, people forgot the poor. Foreigners were mistreated, widows and orphans neglected. Forget God, the prophet inveighed, and you toss ethics out the window. God's reckoning drew near. Catastrophe would befall Jerusalem at the hands of the Babylonian army. Everyone stopped their ears when Jeremiah preached that.

Great risk accompanied him. He was slandered. The temple priest in charge of punishing troublemakers had him beaten, and placed in stocks. He was arrested and sentenced to death, although a wise priest's intervention spared his life. Even Jeremiah's friends and family plotted to murder him. No wonder he resisted the divine pull. At the beginning he protested that youth, and his inability to speak well disqualified him. 'Nonsense', the Almighty responded.

Thus Jeremiah struggled mightily. In our text he laments his vocational plight. This was not the first time. But this speech is unique because he expresses his inability to escape the prophetic calling. It is not only what he does, but who he is in the deepest sense: God's imprint in his mother's womb. Thus the fire in his bones, his innate nature, made it impossible for him to do anything else.

God has claimed your life, just as He claimed Jeremiah's. Your vocation is a calling, something which permeates your being. But there's a cost isn't there? In this viral age, how do you balance protecting loved ones with dangerous demands of your work environment? Can you manage the risks? God will help. Who were you created to be? God will answer. Can you sense the fire in your bones? God will confirm, in stillness, that it is He who sparked the tinder before your birth.

PRAYER:

> Gracious Father I offer thanks. You have purposed me
> to do your will throughout my life. Guard and pro-
> tect me as I risk to help those in need. Be with those
> who labor in hospitals, supermarkets, post offices,
> and restaurants. Be with everyone on the front lines.
> May they be comforted in the knowledge that they're
> making a difference. In the name of our healing Savior
> I pray. Amen.

14

SCRIPTURE:

> "There is great gain godliness and contentment for we brought nothing into this world, and we cannot take anything out of this world, but if we have food and clothing with these we shall be content" 1st Timothy 6:6-7.

In 2008 I traveled to Tanzania to climb Mt. Kilimanjaro. The outfitter was located in the town of Moshi near the peak. Because native guides are very poor, they often take clients like myself up the mountain, wearing little more than sandals and sweatshirts. Kiliminjaro rises 19,360' from the jungle floor, and is frigid on top. Many guides return with severe frostbite, necessitating finger and toe amputation. The local agency helps, but its president asked me if I could muster warm clothing. Any castoff coat, however thread worn, would be appreciated. At the time I served the Kinnelon Reformed Church in New Jersey. The congregation responded, and I left for Africa with a duffel bag stuffed with ski jackets, 15 in all.

One of the great joys of my life was to witness the response of guides and porters as they received coats. I was slated to climb with a group of Europeans. They did not show. Therefore I had a surplus of help: Two guides, two porters, and one cook. Among the group the young cook was my favorite. He received my ski jacket. He beamed. It was as if he had won the lottery. As we descended from the summit, and the temperature rose, I found myself giving away stuff I didn't need: pairs of woolen socks, an extra pair of ski gloves along with baklavas, fleece shirts and tights. Had I donated more, I'd arrive at the Kilimanjaro airport in nothing but a loincloth!

I was repaid for congregational generosity. Before my flight home, the group escorted me in a rickety, overcrowded bus to their small village where we dined on banana goat stew. Because the climb produces a residual hunger, we were all famished the day after our descent, as we gathered inside a hut, and wolfed down the stew. The village was very poor, but they felt it important to sacrifice one of their few goats to feed a stranger. After the meal, the young cook asked me to follow him to a nearby waterfall. It was a 100 foot drop to the small rock hewn pool below. He had taken his ski jacket along, pressed it to his chest, then laid it on a rock, as if it were a sacred garment. Then he ran, and did a 1 ½ somersault before landing dart straight in the small oval. That was his gift for my generosity—a worn ski jacket.

Is contentment easier to discover in this Covid-19 world? We are clothed, and have food. What more do we need? Isn't that salvation? I wonder, too, if the poor have much to teach about gratitude for the basics of life. Their joy gives lie to the idea that happiness arrives only when Covid-19 departs. The days and nights are unnaturally cool this week. My great joy is nestling in overlarge sweatshirts, and sweatpants. In my bundled state, I sense the presence of a warming deity. Then I munch on a Snicker's—God's original power bar, I believe—and all is well with my soul.

PRAYER:

> Heavenly Father, I thank you for providing me with the essentials of life. I thank you for the clothes which keep me warm. I am especially mindful of that old sweater, that familiar coat which comprise my greater family. I thank you for providing me with my 'daily bread'. I pray for the poor in our country, and the impoverished throughout the world. I pray for those who spend countless hours in breadlines, and those whose clothing is insufficient for the weather. Ignite my compassion to care for those who hunger and thirst. I pray that St. John's food pantry will have enough to feed the increased number who arrive at our door. May I do my utmost to secure those in need of basics. In service, help me discover contentment. Amen.

15

SCRIPTURE:

> "The devil led Jesus to Jerusalem and had him stand
> on the highest point of the temple. 'If you are the Son
> of God', he said, 'throw yourself down from here. For
> it is written: 'He will command his angels concerning
> you to guard you carefully; they will lift you up in their
> hands so that you will not strike your foot against a
> stone.' Jesus answered, 'It is said, 'Do not put the Lord
> your God to the test'" Luke 4:9-12.

So begins final temptation during his forty day fast in the wilderness. Satan requests that Jesus becomes a daredevil, launching himself off the pillar of the Temple, a hundred foot drop to the Kidron Valley below. The devil justifies the test by quoting Psalm 91. Let me digress and note the Psalm's relevance for our viral context. In it we read about the, "the pestilence that stalks in the darkness (and) the plague that destroys at midday" (vs. 6). The psalm goes on to state that God will protect us from disease. The devil doesn't quote that verse, but intends another as fulcrum to test God's rescuing ability, and Jesus' need to be rescued. The verse is hopeful. Given very real threat, the angels will catch us if we fall.

But the devil misappropriates the text by asking for a gratuitous act, something which is unnecessary. The request reduces Christ to a daring-do acrobat in a high wire act. No danger, however, if he plummets. In fact he is invited to do just that. For the fun of it. God will provide the safety net. What of God? The Almighty shrinks to sideshow magician, dressed in a top hat and a swallowtail tux, performing tricks for entertainment. Jesus' life is not endangered—unless he accedes, and leaps from the turret. For what reason? For none at all.

What does this event have to do with us? Well, we may know those who affirm that faith will protect them; they need not practice social distancing or face mask wearing. They crow about beach party scrums, and mosh pits. Faith misunderstood also combines with perceptions of beauty—that cloth cover does nothing for the Christian Dior gown. The former must go! God will protect. And churchgoing; well, the Almighty will surround every sanctuary with an antidotal hedge; let's pack 'em in! And, by the way, God dislikes muffled hymn singing; remove the masks and raise the alleluia decibels! Then there's the Christianity-masculinity meld. 'Real men' don't wear masks. Imagine that. In America hyper maleness is defined by the absence of a face covering.

With regard to masculinity, let me quote the words of someone who could outthink and probably, with his burliness and temper, outpunch any non-face mask wearing 'he-man'. He wrote: "I shall ask God to mercifully protect us. Then I shall fumigate, help purify the air, administer medicine, and take it. I shall avoid places and persons where my presence is not needed in order not to be contaminated and thus perchance inflict and pollute others and so cause their death as a result of my negligence...See this is such a God-fearing faith because it is neither brash nor foolhardy and does not TEMPT GOD" (Caps are mine).

The great 16th Century reformer, Martin Luther, penned those words to a fellow scholar during the bubonic plague ravaging Germany. Luther was a good monk who couldn't get right with God, no matter how many hair-shirts he wore, or stone steps bruised knees clomped. Asceticism didn't help, although the young man was convinced it would. Then he perused Paul's letter to the church at Rome, which states that justification before God stems from faith not works, lest boasting occur (3:27). Nonetheless Luther practiced loving acts like the social distancing he refers to above. In the pestilential milieu, he never asks God to relieve him of responsibility for protecting himself and others. He rejects the devil's bait. Angels are not called to swoop with dustpans and brooms. Rather I imagine Luther on his knees for a pragmatic reason, scrubbing the floor with a horsehair brush, and lye soap. May we be just as responsible.

Lord, help me to do my part to end this epidemic. Help me to enact measures to protect others. Help me to express my faith in practical ways. Guide me by your wisdom. Amen.

16

> "As he went along, he saw a man blind from birth. His
> disciples asked him, 'Rabbi, who sinned, this man or
> his parents, that he was born blind?' 'Neither this man
> nor his parents sinned,' said Jesus; he was born blind
> so that God's works might be revealed in him'" John
> 9:1-3.

Jesus' disciples indulged in the blame game. They equated blindness
with sin. Their only question concerned culpability. Did his parents
or the blind man himself transgress? Such thinking erupts whenever
we confront mysterious diseases. During the 14th Century, when
bubonic plague decimated a third of the European population, physicians advised patients to avoid anger before bed. Angry people
were considered contagion vectors. Such thinking resurfaced in rat
infested London of the 16th Century. Immunity lodged in the cheery
personality. In the 18th Century, Dr. Richard Guy wrote, "Women
are more subject to Cancerous Disorders than Men, especially such
Women as are of sedentary and melancholic Disposition of Mind."
In the 19th Century people were reassured that tuberculosis would
not strike as long as they avoided the "melancholic artistic temper-
ment of the age", as one physician wrote.

The 20th Century Spanish flu pandemic produced a dizzying variety of 'sinners' who, putatively, brought the scourge upon themselves—and others. I could go on, but we get the picture. The blame
game accompanies epidemics and diseases. Such thinking promotes
destructive action. In the 14th Century, witches, Jews and other
undesirables were burned at the stake for poisoning wells; the cause
of the epidemic was fouled water as well as pessimistic disposi-
tions. Flash forward to 2020. Riding the subway recently, a Chinese

woman was sprayed with Lysol. It is reported verbal assaults against Asian Americans have risen dramatically. Even if the phrase 'Chinese Virus' was simply informational, the President's words did nothing to breach growing racial tension.

Terror stokes the blame game. We'll never get coronavirus because we know what the sin is, and who the sinners are. We're safe. Note what Jesus avoids. He doesn't answer the disciples' question. Assigning blame produces greater fear and negativity. Rather Jesus states the man's blindness will manifest God's healing glory. It does. Jesus places mud on the man's eyes; he washes in the Pool of Siloam, and sees.

What might our relationship be to coronavirus? Let this scourge become the proving ground for our miracle performing: Healing the lost and lonely by word and deed. Providing support for the infected, who suffer the shame and blame game. Restoring sight to those blinded by anxiety, and pessimism. What if we are the blind man? What if a friend or family member blames us for whatever? Can we forgive because we see clearly anger misplaced? We're an easy target. We're a visible stand-in for the terror our loved ones can't see, or comprehend. We will be compassionate because we understand. And see them. With Christ-like vision.

PRAYER:

> Great God, I thank you for empowering me with your love. Let your spirit of calm abide. In a pestilential world, let my very presence inspire others to seek your peace. Let me reflect your light so that it illuminates the dark corners of frightened souls. May I pronounce hope rather than blame. May I become everything you need me to be. I pray in the name of our healing Savior, Jesus. Amen.

HOLY WEEK

17

SCRIPTURE:

> "Two other men, both, criminals, were also led out
> with him to be executed. When they came to the place
> called the Skull, they crucified him there, along with
> the criminals—one on his right, the other on his left.
> Jesus said, 'Father, forgive them, for they do not know
> what they are doing....Then the criminal said, 'Jesus,
> remember me when you come into your kingdom.'
> Jesus said, 'Truly I tell you, today you will be with me
> in paradise.'" Luke 23:32-34, 42-43.

This Saturday a friend and I cycled 50 miles around our area. The 'Angry Drivers' Club' swells in membership. This was confirmed particularly as we peddled toward Elizaville on East Kerley Corner Road. Horns blared from three cars, although we hugged the gravelly side. Then a truck raced by. The driver swerved toward us, delivering an unremitting honk as he passed. One hundred yards ahead, he braked so that tires squealed, and the pick-up veered. The door opened. We pulled off. Ten long seconds passed before he closed the door, and gunned the engine.

Later my friend said, "I have a confession to make. That guy stopped because I made an obscene gesture. Can you forgive me?" I laughed because such action—though warranted!—was so unlike her. Normally she radiates imperturbability. She never gets rattled. But whatever we know about ourselves comes into question in light of the virus. This weekend I've heard that brawls have broken out in local supermarkets. Covid-19 stokes road rage, and food fights. Perhaps all of us need to be forgiven.

And we are. The Psalmist writes, "God knows how we are formed; He remembers that we are dust" (103:14). As was Jesus. On the cross Our Lord certainly understood our flesh and blood humanity—so under siege in these moments—because he shared it. His human nature was never more transparent than on the cross. Jesus understands how the virus becomes a petri dish for frailty.

We are forgiven without needing to ask. How do I know? Well, the 'repentant thief' never sought pardon from Jesus for the crimes which led to his execution. And they were high crimes indeed. The Greek word, commonly translated as 'thief', can be defined also as 'revolutionary.' Most likely the man whose chest heaved next to Jesus' had Roman blood on his hands. The imperial power had conquered Judea decades before Jesus' birth. There were parties of Jews, known as Zealots, who attempted to liberate their country through violence. Sticking a short dagger into unsuspecting Roman soldiers was the method 'du jure' two thousand years ago. Kill the Roman occupier stealthily. That's why the 'thief' hung from a cross. He says that he and the other insurrectionist deserve their fate; Jesus does not.

The revolutionary's one request is not forgiveness, but remembrance. That's all. 'Think of me as you wing your way to heaven'. 'Recall our time together, and my face perhaps, looking with concern at yours.' Jesus offers more: "Today you will be with me in paradise." Jesus will not abandon his dying companion. Together they'll touch heaven. We are given far more than we petition. Ask to be remembered, and the sky opens. Ask for a backward glance, and we sense His eye-cast throughout our day. Let us go through the present, believing that Christ loves us more than we can comprehend. Let's manage free from guilt. Our Lord stands beside us in our shared and broken humanity. And he beckons us to seek His paradise as we struggle on our crosses.

PRAYER:

Lord Jesus, I've not been myself lately as you well know. I sense your understanding, and your profound empathy borne of your life on earth. Hold me. Secure me. Never forget me. May I have confidence that you will see me through. Help me to sense your presence every moment of every day. Amen.

18

> "Near the cross of Jesus stood his mother, his mother's
> sister, Mary the wife of Clopas, and Mary Magdalene.
> When Jesus saw his mother there, and the disci-
> ple whom he loved standing nearby, he said to her,
> 'Woman, here is your son', and to the disciple, 'Here is
> your mother.' From that time on, this disciple took her
> into his home" John 19:25-27.

No grief is greater than child loss. It subverts the natural order of
life. Children are supposed to outlive their parents. Jesus' mother
watched her son die surrounded by gawkers, and cat-callers. Did
Mary's thoughts range to that first gaze, as Joseph pulled their new-
born from her splayed legs, and placed him, womb fluid slick, on her
chest? Beneath her son's squall, did she keen to his heart thump now
outside and resting above her own before cradling his head, and
laying him in a manger, a feed stall for animals? On Skull Hill, Jesus
appears as naked as the night of his birth. Capital criminals were
not given the luxury of a loincloth, although painters throughout
Christian history have understandably sanitized the blunt scandal
of Roman execution. Nearby Mary stood, woozy with grief. Could
she dare gaze at her own, flesh of her flesh, now transmogrified into
pornography? His body was also hers.

Jesus understood. He intuited, no doubt, the maternal heart rav-
age. He entrusted his mother to the disciple he loved most. And vice
versa. The joining could not be delayed. It came about immediately,
before death stole Messiah's voice. What insight and compassion on
our Lord's part! Jesus' mind should have clamped on his agonies.
Instead he died the way he lived; putting others first.

Imagine John approaching his new mother, hankie in hand,

before her biological son dies. They embrace, their shoulders bob in unison as they weep. What does Jesus' act say to us? When a loved one dies, our Lord beckons us to start over, the sooner the better. We should grieve. The price we pay for loving deeply is profound mourning. Together they mark our full humanity. Ongoing grief is meant to deepen our faith, and draw us closer to our Lord. That's why Jesus stated in better times, "Blessed are those who mourn, for they shall be comforted" (Matthew 5:4).

Jesus' pronouncement from the cross, at the height of Mary's grief, counters the idea that the capacity to love again occurs only after sorrow has ebbed or passed. There has to be 'closure' before moving on. We infer from the text that grief and love need not be sequential. It's better for us if they're not. Mary's mourning continues, I'm sure, but now she has another son who needs her care. Perhaps it is the power of mourning itself which opens the heart, like a pantry door, to new attachment, and new love. Grieving's yowl hollows the soul, so that its obverse— passion can flood the void. Not acknowledging and wrestling with grief prevents love's full incursion.

In keeping with our text can we be like Jesus the Matchmaker? In our Covid-19 world, as newscasts alert us to rising death tolls, we are called to ask: Who has lost a mother and needs another ASAP? What about a father, spouse, or child? On the cross Jesus dispels the myth that we can't, or shouldn't, love again. It's a message worth proclaiming even to ourselves.

PRAYER:

> Lord open my being so that I can grieve and love
> simultaneously if need be. Surround me with your
> compassion this day. Even if I am weighted by viral
> fears, let me know I am safe with you, and that your
> empowerment provides strength to create new couples
> and families. In the name of my healing Savior I pray.
> Amen.

19

> "At noon, darkness came over the whole land until
> three in the afternoon. And at three in the afternoon
> Jesus cried out in a loud voice, 'Eloi, Eloi, lama sabach-
> thani' which means, 'My God, my God, why have you
> forsaken me?'" Mark 15:33-34.

Both Matthew and Mark record Jesus' agonizing words from the cross. They seem appropriate given our present situation. Have we uttered his cry of dereliction ourselves recently? Or have we in the past, burdened by another tragedy? If we've been there, carrying whatever cross life has dealt, does atheism skirt the mind? A famous 19th Century philosopher, Ludwig Feuerbach, once noted that theology is anthropology writ large: Prayer simply invokes a human ideal, projected skyward. There is nothing more. The heavens are empty, except for our reflection. Decades later Sigmund Freud wrote much the same. 'God' is nothing more than the heavenward placement of an idealized father.

Jesus' words contravene Feuerbach and Freud. Our Lord doesn't say, 'If you exist, why am I abandoned?' 'If there is a God, why has this tragedy happened to me?' 'If there is a just and loving presence in the universe, why do innocents suffer?' Jesus does not philosophize. He personalizes. He addresses 'My God... You are my God, and not an abstraction. You are my God who I have known and served.' The wrenching question belongs to a son who loves his father, and cannot fathom the parent's seeming abandonment. It is pleading to one he has always trusted and heretofore understood. Thus the cry of the crucified is not speculative; it is intimate.

The 20th Century theologian, Joachim Jeremias, first understood the importance of Jesus' use of the Hebrew word, 'Abba' rather than 'Ab' when referring to God. 'Abba' means 'Dad' or 'Daddy'. A righteous Jew in Jesus' day might use the diminutive to speak to a father but never as address to the Almighty. 'Ab', or 'Father' was the proper word for prayer. To use 'Abba' in synagogue or Temple seemed blasphemous. This is the word Jesus uses.

On the cross he never doubted his Dad's love for him. In his despair, however, he felt abandoned. For a moment. His forsakenness would be engulfed by God's loving presence. How do I know? On the cross, Jesus was able to forgive his executioners and entrust his mother to her new son, the author of John's Gospel. We may feel orphaned during the pandemic, but God will continue to work His acts of love in and through us just as he did through Jesus.

There's a second interpretation of our Lord's words from the cross. It need not replace the first. One can balance both. As a youngster, the first Psalm I learned was the 23rd: "The Lord is my shepherd…" My parents read it and Sunday School taught it. Two thousand years ago, Psalm 22 took precedence in a child's learning. It begins, "My God, my God, why hast thou forsaken me?" It ends, as many Psalms do, on notes of triumph and hope. On the cross Jesus may have recited the psalm he memorized as a little boy. Perhaps the crowd heard only its beginning, as Jesus' voice soon waned. Psalm 22, and its trajectory, that abandonment would transmute to praise, imprinted itself early, calming the child on the cross.

PRAYER:

> God increase my faith during these difficult times.
> Overcome my doubt, my turmoil, and soothe so that I
> may affirm anew that you are my Dad, and that your
> love will bring me safely through this dark period. In
> the name of our healing Savior I pray. Amen.

20

SCRIPTURE:
> "Later, knowing that everything had now been finished,
> and so that the Scripture would be fulfilled, Jesus said,
> 'I am thirsty.' A jar of wine vinegar was there, so they
> soaked a sponge in it, put a sponge on the stalk of the
> hyssop plant and lifted it to Jesus' lips" John 19:28-29.

Given his predicament, I wonder if vinegar tasted like the finest wine to our Lord. On Thursday evening Jesus celebrated the last Passover with his disciples. I bet the redolence of roasted lamb sent them into a gustatory swoon as it was placed on the table. Even the bitter herbs of that sacred feast may have seemed delicious. Under threat of Jesus' imminent death, I believe the gifts of smell and taste magnified. Perhaps it's always been that way. In Nazi concentration camps, survivors endured by conjuring the aromas and flavors of favorite foods. In his book, "Man's Search for Meaning" survivor Viktor Frankl noted that a favorite pastime was swapping recipes. The activity kept the prisoners sane, and hopeful.

I believe God uses dire situations to heighten olfactory, and taste senses. God wants us to thrive rather than survive. Last evening I stood over pan seared scallops, resting in a skillet as their juice mingled with Pernod, and chilled butter to thicken. Heaven on earth. There is a Buddhist tale about a tiger chasing a man over a cliff. The fellow grasps a root on the sheer wall. He looks down at a thousand foot drop. He looks up and sees the tiger licking its lips. He looks to the side and spots a ripe strawberry. He plucks, sniffs, and pops it into his mouth. Then he says to himself, 'This is the best day of my life.' God wants us to have such days in the midst of Covid-19.

Jesus' words from the cross also fulfill Scripture in two ways. First, in Psalm 69:21 we read, "They put gall in my food and gave

me vinegar for my thirst." Everything Jesus says fulfills prophecy.
Second, the mention of hyssop hints at ressurection. The night before
liberation from Egypt, the Angel of Death spared the firstborn of the
Hebrews because the lintels of their huts were daubed with lamb's
blood. Hyssop was the 'paint brush'. The long stemmed plant's
'cameo' in John alerts us to the imminent upturn in human history.
Jesus will die, but the Angel of death will not take permanent possession. It will pass by a borrowed tomb outside Jerusalem. Hyssop
indicates subtly the resurrection to come. During Holy Week, may
we discover divine clues which point to our ultimate liberation from
this epidemic.

PRAYER:

> Great God, help me discover daily joys. Let me
> approach my meals with deep gratitude, and delight.
> Help me to imagine your future when I'll eat and drink
> again with people outside my home, folks I love and
> miss. In Christ's healing name I pray. Amen.

21

SCRIPTURE:

> "When he had received the drink, Jesus said, 'It is
> finished.' With that, he bowed his head and gave up his
> spirit" John 19:30.

Traditionally this day has been called Good Friday. Jesus' dying seems anything but good. Here he pronounces sad valediction to his ministry and life. The 19th Century poet, Algernon Swineburn, wrote, "O, Pale Galilean, the world has grown cold with thy breath." We imagine the messiah's parting words sent a chill to those who watched their beloved die at Golgotha, 'Skull Hill'. His wracked body confirmed his words. Everything ended that day. The hopes and dreams of his healing and teaching ministry. The good news he proclaimed to the lost, grieving and persecuted. The hopes of the approaching Kingdom of God. All now as inert and unmoving as his wrist-bones, iron nail staked.

This is the traditional understanding of Christ's final words. Let's look closer. The sentence "It is finished" translates from the single Greek word, 'tetelesthai.' Another definition, 'It is accomplished,' is far more positive. Suppose Jesus shouts victory before he dies? It is accomplished: 'I've done everything needed to bring hope to the world.' It is accomplished: 'I've taken your sins upon my broken body, so that you might be washed clean by my blood.' It is accomplished: 'I've demonstrated you can forgive your enemies, and possess 'executive functioning'— "Woman, here is your son...here is your mother"—in the midst of suffering.'

The second definition finds support in another setting. A runner would shout the word when he crossed the finish line first. It is likely that the apostle Paul heard the victory cry when he established a church in Corinth, since it hosted the Isthmus Games, second in importance to the Olympics. Unlike its famous counterpart, city streets in Corinth became the route marathoners took. They may have jogged by Paul's residence. Although we infer from Scripture he was no athlete himself, he uses the racing metaphor to describe the nature of triumphant faith (1 Corinthians 9:24-26). He mentions running in other letters as well (Galatians 2:2, 5:17; Philippians 2:16; 2Timothy 4:7).

We return to the cross once more before Easter. In this grim scene can we imagine hope? I think so. Watch as Christ's breath quickens. His legs straighten, pushing away from the cross. His back arches, lifting his chest to heaven. He roars, 'tetelesthai', deafening bystanders, and swerving bird flight. In the late 1st Century, writers referred to Christian martyrs as 'athletes'. Peter and Paul were described later as such because, it was assumed, they had died in Rome, during Nero's persecution of Christians in 64 AD. Jesus, too, was an athlete. He sprinted across God's finish line as he shouted victory from the cross.

Can we shout 'tetelesthai' when we have completed the self-sacrificial work God has entrusted to us this day? Before we go to sleep on this Good Friday evening, may we pray, 'Lord this day I've accomplished your will in spite of suffering. I feel joy because I have overcome all obstacles.' And as sleep closes our eyes, may we hear Christ whisper, "Well done, my good and faithful servant."

PRAYER:

> Healing Savior, love of my life, may I become more like you. Increase my confidence that you are working in and through me to bring hope to those who are frightened, and to those who suffer. Use me as you see fit. I am yours fully and completely. Amen.

EASTER

22

SCRIPTURE:

"When the Sabbath was over, Mary Magdalene, Mary
the mother of James, and Salome bought spices so that
they might go to anoint Jesus' body. Very early on
the first day of the week, just after sunrise, they were
on their way to the tomb and they asked each other,
'Who will roll the stone away from the entrance of the
tomb?' But when they looked up, they saw that the
stone, which was very large, had been rolled away. As
they entered the tomb, they saw a young man dressed
in a white robe sitting on the right side, and they were
alarmed. But he said to them, 'Do not be alarmed; you
are looking for Jesus of Nazareth, who was crucified.
He has been raised; he is not here. Look, there is the
place they laid him. But go tell his disciples, and Peter
that he is going ahead of you to Galilee; there you will
see him, just as Nothe told you.' So they went out and
fled from the tomb, for terror and amazement had
seized them; and they said nothing to anyone, for they
were afraid" Mark 16:1-8.

Mark is the earliest Gospel and his description of the resurrection
the shortest. Absent are visual appearances of Christ. In Matthew's
Gospel, the disciples spend time with Jesus on a mountain top in
Galilee. In Luke he accompanies two as they walk toward the village
of Emmaus. They recognize him after he breaks bread at supper.
Then Jesus appears to others sheltering in Jerusalem. After appear-
ances in the capital, the Lord encounters his disciples by the Sea of
Galilee in John's Gospel.

Because Jesus doesn't appear in Mark, we glean no comforting sayings unlike the other three. The women arrive at the empty tomb and are struck dumb. Only an angel speaks. Most disturbing is Mark's ending. The women flee from the tomb terrorized. That's it. The End. Not the conclusion worthy of a Hollywood Jesus movie. Even the early church felt unease. Additional endings were added so that the 2nd Evangelist conformed to the other three Gospel writers. Throughout Christian history, Mark's abbreviation brought concern, if not bewilderment, to the faithful. Well into the 20th Century, several New Testament scholars theorized that his final page had been lost.

Interestingly literary critics, in recent times, speculate that the finish aligns more closely to contemporary short fiction than Mark's literary milieu. His account raises questions. It does not end neatly. Suspense is raised because, absent of the other three Gospels, one wonders whether the women will return to Galilee. Finally, and most critically, the account ends in fear instead of rosy resurrection proclamations.

In this Covid-19 period, Mark's ending resonates with our fright infused thinking, or non-thinking. The rattled women flee 'Good news'. Do we? Has terror overwhelmed to such degree that we can't hear glad tidings of resurrection, even if an angel placed bullhorns next to our ears? Do we focus on tombs, empty or otherwise, instead of a messenger who speaks of a hopeful future. God understands our predicament, and will calm our fears. Just ask when anxiety spikes, entering a busy supermarket or fleeing an unmasked cougher. On this Easter Sunday, God will cast out anxiety and restore your belief in Christ's resurrection. If the Father raised his Son from death, it's no big deal to resuscitate flagging belief.

What God asks is what the angel announced to the women. Once fear un-grips, return to Galilee. Galilee is the region where Christ grew up and began his ministry. The territory is roughly 100 miles north of Jerusalem. Where is Galilee for us? It may be the geography where we, like the disciples, first encountered Jesus. Was it at home where a channel surf led, unintendedly, to a preacher who said exactly what you needed to hear? Perhaps it occurred at church, the very last place you wanted to be. Your loved one nearly slapped a chloroform mask over your face to get you through the sanctuary door. Maybe a picnic, or a stroll in a field to 'catch some rays'. What you caught was God's tender spirit. A crib symbolized Galilee for me. I was in it at the time. My first inference ever was that the light beam behind the smiling maternal face was not my mother. It was Christ.

On this strange Easter Sunday, filled with viral fear, may we remember our Galilees. The angel calls us. Can we overcome the psychic paralysis Covid-19 induces, and recollect the sacred geography of our being on this holiest of days? Most certainly.

PRAYER:

> Loving Father, help me to experience the joys of this resurrection day. May my soul bring forth Alleluias so that the earth and sky resound with my praise. Guide me back to that time and place, where I knew no fear, and where I experienced your security and love. Help me to guide others as they trace their sacred origins. In the name of my precious Savior, Jesus, I pray. Amen.

SCRIPTURE:

> "Now Mary stood outside the tomb crying. As she
> wept, she bent over to look into the tomb and saw
> two angels in white, seated where Jesus' body had
> been, one at the head and the other at the foot. They
> asked her, 'Woman, why are you crying?' 'They have
> taken my Lord away,' she , 'and I don't know where
> they have put him.' At this, she turned around and
> saw Jesus standing there, but she didn't realize that it
> was Jesus. He asked her, 'Woman, why are you crying?
> Who is it you are looking for?' Thinking he was the
> gardener, she said, 'Sir, if you have carried him away,
> tell me where you have put him, and I will get him.'
> Jesus said to her, 'Mary.'" John 20:11-18.

This is the most dramatic scene in the resurrection narratives. We know little about Mary. She encountered Jesus early in his ministry when he cast out seven demons from her (Luke 8:2). The number represented fullness back then. Today she might be classified as psychotic. Her last name, Magdalene, may derive from Magdala, a fishing village on the Sea of Galilee. Apart from the Gospels, she is never mentioned in the New Testament. In the former, however, her name appears 12 times, more than most of Jesus' male disciples, and more than any other non-family woman. After the 1st Century she emerges in a number of non-canonical gospels, one which bears her name. In the Gospel of Mary, she encourages Jesus' fearful followers, "The son of man is within you, follow him." In this and other writings Mary is the one who knows Jesus best.

In 591 Pope Gregory the 1st smirches Mary's character in several Easter sermons. He conflates her with Mary of Bethany (Luke

10:39), and the unnamed sinful woman who anoints Jesus' feet in Luke 7:36-50. I don't believe that Mary was a prostitute, but let's assume for a moment she was. Jesus' closest female follower had additional baggage to say the least. How do you put 'former crazy person and sex worker' in a resume? You don't. Can we imagine the caterwauls from villages Jesus and his followers entered, and quickly exited? The fact that she was formerly demon possessed was bad enough. Coming from a lakeside town word spread rapidly to other towns in the vicinity. She may have been healed, but it was more enjoyable for gossips to unearth her past. I imagine she still felt the demonic weight, although Jesus had lifted it from her.

I bet shame burdened particularly as she stood near the cross. It surfaced again near the empty tomb. The 19th Century philosopher Friedrich Nietzsche wrote, "When we are tired, we are attacked by ideas we conquered long ago." Perhaps Magdalene represents us in this respect. Overwhelmed by tragedy, our tendency is to dredge up our failings. Indeed Christ has set us free from sin, and from the past. Nevertheless contagion has the power to weaken faith so that, with time on our hands, we can tick off a transgressional laundry list. I believe Mary did this until Christ's resurrected presence halted her slide. We observe the Covid-19 cross. And the empty tomb. Christ negates the weight of painful pasts. His moment to moment love for us will blot out what has gone before, and inscribe lovingly what is yet to be.

PRAYER:

> Jesus, strengthen my faith this day. It's easy to focus on the past when I didn't meet my expectations, let alone yours. Forgiveness has become an intellectual proposition. I don't feel it in my gut, where it belongs. Let me experience your affirming presence this day, this moment. Amen.

24

SCRIPTURE:

> "Thinking he was the gardener, she said, 'Sir, if you
> have carried him away, tell me where you have put
> him, and I will get him.' Jesus said to her, 'Mary.' She
> turned toward him and cried out, 'Rabboni!' (which
> means 'Teacher'). Jesus said, 'Do not hold on to me,
> for I have not yet ascended to the Father. Go instead
> to my brothers and tell them, 'I am ascending to my
> Father, and your Father, to my God and your God.'
> Mary Magdalene went to the disciples with the news,
> 'I have seen the Lord!' And she told them that he had
> said these things to her" John 20:15-18.

This is the sequel to yesterday's meditation. Interestingly Jesus practices 'social distancing' two millennia ago. Our Lord prevents Mary from hugging him. The prohibition does not dilute their profound feeling. That's a lesson for us. So often we believe that physical contact with the beloved deepens our relationship, and most often it does. But in our body beautiful, sexualized culture, physicality can short circuit the verbal care loving relationships require. Covid-19 forces us to express our feelings by carefully choosing words to convey our deepest emotions. Heart-speak only enhances a hug.

On Easter Sunday I called Lily, my youngest daughter. She lives in Eugene, Oregon. She's accepted the fact that I don't face time with her, largely because I have a primitive's fear of seeing myself. Plus now, with my unshorn locks, I'll soon resemble a scraggly 30,000 year old Neanderthal—not a pretty sight! We spoke simply and lovingly over the phone. The same with Sarah, my oldest. What needed to be said was. Love blossomed. My middle daughter, Joanna, texted her Easter greetings. She put thought in what she tapped on her cell. One particular sentence caused my heart to reel with joy.

I treasure several love letters my father wrote my mother while they were courting. He saw her across a crowded room one New Year's Eve. My father's mother had forced his sister to take her kid brother to the party—a good thing for me! My parents always held hands, waltzed, and hugged. His letters conveyed the soul sounding depths of his passion. I wish I had been there as he penned those missives. I wish I had been there when Jesus uttered Mary's name.

PRAYER:

> Lord, should I write a love letter to someone who
> needs to understand the fullness of my love? Should I
> surprise that someone if he or she lives under my roof?
> Help me to express clearly what my heart longs to say.
> Let my love, well written, and spoken, alleviate the fear
> my loved one feels. In your healing name I pray. Amen.

25

SCRIPTURE:

> "Now Thomas (also known as Didymus), one of the
> Twelve, was not with the disciples when Jesus came. So
> the other disciples told him, 'We have seen the Lord!'
> But he said to them, 'Unless I see the nail marks in the
> hands, and put my finger where the nails were, and put
> my hand into his side, I will not believe.' A week later
> his disciples were in the house again, and Thomas was
> with them. Though the doors were locked, Jesus came
> and stood among them and said, 'Peace be with you!'
> Then he said to Thomas, 'Put your finger here, and
> see my hands. Reach out your hand and put it into my
> side. Stop doubting and believe.' Thomas said to him,
> 'My Lord and my God!' Then Jesus told him, 'Because
> you have seen me, you have believed; blessed are
> those who have not seen, and yet have believed'" John
> 20:24-29.

Poor Thomas. The moniker 'Doubting' precedes his name throughout Christian history. The other disciples share his doubt, although
they are less forthcoming. Matthew tells us that they went to Galilee,
to the mountain which their resurrected Lord directed: "When they
saw him they worshiped him, but some doubted"(28:17). Luke
notes that Jesus appears to them in a Jerusalem room. The Savior
announces, "Peace" to his followers. Their response is just the opposite: "They were startled and frightened, thinking they saw a ghost."
Jesus asks, "Why are you troubled, and why do doubts rise in your
mind?" (24:36-38). Back to John's Gospel. A few sentences later he
extends Thomas' request to the others. Touch the wounds of his
body so that they'll know he is more than a ghost.

Doubting is intrinsic to the Gospel accounts. In his work, 'Purity of Heart is to Will One Thing', the 19th Century philosopher, Soren Kierkegaard, noted that it is easier for the 'second hand believer'— you and me—than it was for the earliest followers who witnessed the actual event; our historical 'distancing' aids faith. I disagree with the Danish theologian. Jesus says as much in our present text today: "Blessed are those who have not seen, and yet have believed." So Christ understands our difficulty. He realizes our modern day vantage makes faith more difficult. Now toss in Covid-19.

Doubt stipples humanity. Kierkegaard's 'first hand' 'second hand' distinction blurs when we read about the father who asks Jesus to cure his demon possessed boy. Jesus tells the man that everything is possible for one who believes. The stricken dad states, "I believe, help thou my unbelief" (Mark 9:24). That's us in a nutshell. Our day to day journey is marked by ambivalence. And the father's ambivalence does not prevent our Lord from healing his son. Nor can Christ's love for us be mitigated by wavering faith.

Has Covid-19 increased your doubts about the resurrection? Has the daily death toll blunted the 'Allelulias' you raised on Easter? Don't worry. Jesus understands. When you express your doubts to the Messiah, He will prove to you, as he did to his earliest followers, that He's as real today as He was two thousand years ago. Because we are 'second hand believers' Christ may not appear in the flesh. But he will manifest himself in our flesh, causing hearts to skip and minds to light.

Can doubt be something positive? Yes and no. No, certainly when it is perpetual (James 1:6), or when it is unmoored from the existential crises one faces. The person who has no 'skin in the game', who doubts because it is fashionable intellectually to do so is an example of the latter. Doubt blesses however, when it produces the faith of our 'Doubting Thomas'. Thomas struggles. He demands proof. Whether or not he actually pokes Christ's stigmata is moot. At the end Thomas makes the greatest statement of faith in the New Testament: "My Lord, and my God." Reality is sufficiently difficult that belief-wrestling marks, or should mark, the Christian journey.

And that's positive because, like Thomas, sturdy faith derives from God grappling.

PRAYER:

> Healing Jesus, my Savior, transform my doubt into greater faith. Work in me as you worked in Thomas. Still my mind so that I might sense your spirit working in and through me. Give me confidence to know that you are with me in the present, and will guide me in the future. I love you. I trust you. You are my Lord and my God. Amen.

26

SCRIPTURE:

> "For if the dead are not raised, then Christ has not been raised either. And if Christ has not been raised, your faith is futile; you are still in your sins. Then those who have fallen asleep in Christ are lost. If only in this life we have hope in Christ, we are of all people most to be pitied. But Christ indeed has been raised from the dead, the first fruits of those who have fallen asleep. For since death came through a man, the resurrection of the dead comes also through a man. For as in Adam all die, so in Christ all will be made alive" 1st Corinthians 15:16-22.

What does the resurrection mean for us? Paul explains in his first letter to the church he founded. Christ's resurrection portends our own. Not even death can separate us from the love of Christ as the Apostle mentions in another epistle (Romans 8:38). But how can we be sure? This article falls under greater scrutiny as we scan mortality rates, and watch refrigerated trucks turn to morgues. Does Covid-19 shake faith? You bet.

That's why Jesus keeps reappearing after he leaves the tomb, to remind and reassure. 'I'm alive' he demonstrates in word and deed to his frightened followers. 'And you will be, too, for eternity.' Jesus' statement at the Last Supper is poignant: "Do not let your hearts be troubled. Believe in God, believe also in me. In my Father's (heavenly) house are many rooms; if it were not so would I have told you that I go to prepare a place for you, and if I go to prepare a place for you, I will come again and take you to myself, that where I am you may also be" (John 14:1-3).

The great 13th Century Dominican theologian, Thomas Aquinas, proofed the existence of God, and thereby future hope of resurrection. His five step treatise may not grab us today. More simply, we need ask only, 'In our heart of hearts, do we believe death is the end?' Or does our core affirm the opposite? Intellectually we may believe in extinction. Science seems to back this. So do philosphers. Mortality is the natural terminus; nothing more proceeds. What do our emotions intimate? If dying were as natural as we are told often, why does the thought, well, scare us to death? I like Woody Allen's statement: "I'm not afraid to die; I just don't want to be around when it happens." Can we dismiss the adage, 'There are no atheists in foxholes.' Sure we can, if we're not cowering in a trench under enemy fire. But the fear of death can't be dismissed. Not among soldiers I've had the honor to meet, who've fought on front lines. The apostle Paul calls death, "the last enemy"(1st Corinthians 15:26). More graphically, the poet Yeats refers to it as the "Ruffian on the Stairs." Both descriptions are apt.

Ecclesiastes states that God has placed "eternity in our hearts" (3:11). The writer suggests that something God-given nests within. Eternal life as instinct. Even atheists may grumblingly admit that people long for eternity. Writing after the carnage of World War 1, Sigmund Freud noted, "It is indeed impossible to imagine our own death; and whenever we attempt to do so, we can perceive that we are, in fact, still spectators." Death and dying expert, Avery Wiseman wrote in a similar vein "…most dying patients still cling to an image of survival which promises to preserve their unique, distinctive consciousness." That's what Christianity offers: Rekindled consciousness along with a spiritual body to boot!

Perhaps Christianity triumphed over competing religions in the ancient world because of the specifics of post-mortem existence. Take Stoicism, for example. Its philosophy held that one's essence would meld with the stars, or planets becoming one with a harmonic universe. Eternality in a sense, but one which lacks individual consciousness. It's romantic, and akin to folks who tell me they look forward to enriching the soil with their remains. And it may be the truth. Faith is faith after all, and no one, in my life, has returned from the dead. There are moments of doubt for me. Death frightens, especially at this time. I'd rather not expire, just yet, under Covid-19's watch.

Tolstoy wrote a novella, "The Death of Ivan Ilyich." Ivan is a bureaucrat on the move until he is stricken with terminal illness. As he lay dying, he remembers the syllogism learned in grade school logic class: 'All men are human; all men must die. I am human; therefore I must die.' Ivan protests. The deduction applies to man in the abstract. That he is not! He is special because his mother dandled him on her knee. He had a pet, and loving family. In essence, Ivan assures himself, he may be human, but he was not meant to die, no matter what an elementary school syllogism maintains. He is too special for that, his being cries.

So are we. Beyond this life God has other plans for us. Believe it. Let the ingrained resurrection hope wing you through this pandemic.

PRAYER:

> God, I have known someone who has died because of this scourge. Friends have told me about their friends who have passed. Help me to offer hope to those who mourn, and comfort for those who are gravely ill. In word and deed help me to lift the banner of eternal life for all. Lord, make me a resurrection restorer this day. Amen.

SCRIPTURE:

> "Now that same day two of them were going to a village called Emmaus, about seven miles from Jerusalem. They were talking with each other about everything that had happened. As they talked and discussed these things with each other, Jesus himself came up and walked along with them, but they were kept from recognizing him. He asked them, 'What are you discussing together as you walk along?' They stood still, their faces downcast. One of them, named Cleopas, asked him, 'Are you the only visiting Jerusalem who does not know the things that have happened there in these days?' 'What things?' he asked. 'About Jesus of Nazareth,' they replied. 'He was a prophet, powerful in word and deed before God and all the people. The chief priests and our rulers handed him over to be sentenced to death, and they crucified him; but we had hoped that he was the one who was going to redeem Israel'" Luke 24:13-21.

Thus begins Luke's 'Road to Emmaus' account about two disciples fleeing Jerusalem in despair. They encounter Jesus, but do not recognize him. In the Gospel of John, as well as our text, a veiled Christ meets his followers after resurrection. Let me suggest a therapeutic reason why. He understood the disciples' need to be sad. The cross ended a loving relationship. Jesus had become their dearest friend as well as teacher. His death also negated all hope that their master was the sword wielding generalissimo who would liberate Israel from Roman occupation. The two disciples grieved their personal loss as well as Jewish expectation of what a warrior messiah would accomplish.

In better times, Jesus pronounced, "Blessed are those who mourn, for they will be comforted" (Matthew 5:4). Jesus disguises so that the duo can mourn fully. In the Gospel of John he appears as a stranger so that Mary Magdalene can weep. (John 20:15-16). Jesus reveals himself only after she is prostrate with grief. Therapists understand that it is much easier to discuss sorrows with a stranger than with someone intimately known. The stranger can be more objective, reacting less to despair than a loved one might. A therapeutic relationship is compromised when a client's pain triggers something within the therapist which damages his or her helping orientation. It happens.

As a counselor I understand also that most clients can appropriate hope after despair is voiced. Jesus asks why they are sad. He certainly knows. But he is their faithful therapist. To have revealed himself too early would have forestalled the depths of full throated anguish.

The Lord serves as our model. Be the listening ear to anyone whose great heart-ache causes his or her face to blush. Perhaps one mourns the ending of a job, or business. Maybe there's spousal dying, magnified by the closed doors of the ICU, preventing final good-byes. Perhaps the individual quakes because he or she serves on the front lines in the Covid-19 war. Attune yourself carefully, and lovingly. Avoid the 'jolly up' method of counseling. It doesn't work. We are called to empathize profoundly with cruciform stories, before offering hopeful news. If one understands that he or she has been heard, accepted, and loved by us, be assured that Christ's resurrecting presence will do the rest.

PRAYER:

> Lord make me an instrument of your compassionate
> presence as I walk through this valley of the shadow.
> Draw people to me because they understand I possess
> a listening ear and caring heart. Fill me with joy as I
> perform the tasks you call me to accomplish. Amen.

28

SCRIPTURE:

> "'I'm going out to fish,' Simon Peter told them, and they
> said, 'We'll go with you.' So they went out and got into
> the boat, but that night they caught nothing. Early in
> the morning, Jesus stood on the shore, but the disciples
> did not realize that it was Jesus. He called out to them,
> 'Friends haven't you any fish?' 'No', they answered"
> John 21:3-5.

Bad news precedes good. Before Jesus directs the disciples to haul a miraculous catch, their nets yield nothing after hours of toil. Some scholars suggest the disciples returned to Galilee to escape the twin shocks of crucifixion and resurrection. It wasn't simply our Lord's execution. The Gospels record that even Jesus' reappearance terrified them. Early in the 20th Century biochemist Hans Selye wrote about good stress, as well as 'distress', the latter held the same meaning for him as it does for us. For Selye, good stress frightens also. Thus resurrection, along with crucifixion, palpitated hearts.

The disciples' fear pursued them 100 miles north away from death/ resurrection in Jerusalem. If they could have flown to Timbuktu, their terrors would have boarded as well. Maybe they understood fear's persistence. Let me speculate that experienced fishermen couldn't figure out the difference between the fore and aft of their boat, let alone intuit the location of fish, something they could have done easily in their sleep. Terror submerged reasoning. We're like the disciples. Fear may prevent us from doing our best work. We may be 'slower on the uptake'. Anxiety attacks and vitiates resolve.

In this Covid-19 age, self-condemnation prevails. What's wrong with us?, we wonder. Well the impinging epidemic is what's wrong. Not you. God understands you're doing your best under extraordinary circumstances. God wants us to be gentle with ourselves. No self-flagellation if your goals—or shoals for that matter—go unmet.

Among good and faithful people, I often discover expectations run higher than present capability during this period. That's not bad in itself. It's better to reach beyond our grasp than to bend the arm, unless, of course, the former unleashes an unhealthy dose of negative thinking when we fail to meet expectation and begin to self-lacerate. Stop condemning yourself. God knows you're not a slacker. He understands the overwhelming demands of a coronavirus day. Continue to work hard. Keep at it, even if once easily achieved goals now elude. 'Cut yourself some slack', it's said. Didn't Jesus speak those very words? "Beloved, cut thyself some slack." Well, I believe he meant it even if he didn't say it. It should be Gospel for all of us.

PRAYER:

> Jesus, you know I'm doing my best. Although life is far from normal these days, sometimes I fool myself thinking that it is. I often condemn myself because I cannot manage responsibilities the way I did before the pandemic. Help me to understand the psychological burden Covid-19 places. Help me to relax, and do what I can. Let me abide in your love this day. Amen.

29

SCRIPTURE:

"Jesus said to them, 'Come and have breakfast.'" John 21:13.

The resurrected Lord cooks breakfast for his disciples on the shore of the Sea of Galilee. When we think about it, Jesus' important work occurs at meals. In Luke's 'Road to Emmaus' story, the disciples no longer see a stranger, but Jesus himself as he breaks bread with them. At table Jesus commends Mary for listening while her sister, Martha, scurries to prepare dinner for the teacher. Teaching ensues after Jesus feeds the crowds, multiplying loaves and fishes. At dinner, in the home of a Simon, a woman anoints Jesus' feet with oil. And it is at the beginning of our Lord's work that he changes water into wine at a wedding feast in Cana of Galilee. In our present text, after breakfast Jesus lifts Peter's guilt, so that he can lead the nascent church when the Holy Spirit arrives at Pentecost.

Perhaps eating and teaching go hand in hand. We are more receptive at the dinner table because we are truly ourselves when drawn butter dribbles to our chin, munching that third ear of corn. The story is told of an elderly woman about to meet her Maker. She was asked what she would like in her casket, "Only this," she said to her friend. She held out a table spoon from the church. "When I was a little girl, I was told at every church pot luck dinner, to hold on to my spoon because the best was yet to come. And it was. Dessert! So I will die with my spoon because I know the best is yet to come!"

Meaningful discussion occurs over dinner. Might Covid-19 change our atomizing pre-pandemic understanding of what eating together means? I hope so. Often meals become grab and go affairs. Our cheeks swell as we stuff whatever in our mouths, racing to the next event. I'm exaggerating. A little. Will the quarantine return us to simpler, slower pleasures?

Do we have time now to say the things which need to be said? Can we restore loving intimacy as we pass the chicken and mashed potatoes? Of course intimacy derives even when we're not talking around the table. In 2016, I spent two weeks in a monastery where all meals were taken in silence. I never felt closer to the monks when chewing was the only sound heard. Indeed I never felt closer to myself. Let's deepen our love by the thoughtful way we gather at table.

PRAYER:

> Lord help me to slow down so that I can express gratitude for the food I eat, and the loved ones with whom I share. Amen.

30

_____

SCRIPTURE:

> "Jesus said, 'I am the true vine, and my father is the
> gardener. He cuts off every branch in me which bears
> no fruit, while every branch which does bear fruit he
> prunes so that it will be even more fruitful...I am the
> vine and you are the branches. If you remain in me,
> and I in you, you will bear much fruit'" John 15:1-2, 5.

Jesus' words are part of his farewell discourse to his disciples, shortly
before he is arrested, tried and executed. He speaks about bearing
fruit at a time wrought with fear and danger. A time like ours. In the
midst of Covid-19 we, too, are called to fructify. The pandemic may
sharpen our understanding of what needs to be pruned.

Twenty years ago I spent an afternoon with a vintner whose grape
fields roll to the shore of Lake Geneva in Switzerland. He showed
me a vine, the size of a medicine ball, which had been pruned time
and again so that it was able to produce luscious grapes. It was not
the prettiest object to look at, but it was highly effective in creating
what it was meant to create. The vintner noted that the vine was
strong because it had 'survived tough seasons'. Decades ago I had
the misfortune of stumbling upon two women from the South, argu-
ing the merits of Texas grapefruit versus those grown in Florida. The
Texan won when she noted that 'her' grapefruit survived tougher
winters.

Perhaps our present day scourge provides backdrop for Christ's
pruning work on us. In the light of Covid-19, it may be easier to
see aspects of ourselves which need lopping. Maybe it's resent-
ment. Maybe it's shearing off individuals whose 'job' it is to hurt
us. Maybe it's a view of reality which does not comport with reality:
We're either too negative, and cynical, or we occupy the antipode,

singing a happy tune in moments when reality requires a dirge. Then there's the delicate balance our Lord calls us to maintain. He states, "Be wise as serpents and innocent as doves" (Matthew 10:16). Are we too naive to assess the viral threat accurately, and thereby pose a threat to ourselves and others? Or are we too 'serpent-like', thinking we can figure things out apart from divine help, or, indeed, help from others?

God can use our viral strait to bring us closer to Christ, our Vine, and faithful redeemer. May we be grateful for the pruning which occurs during this tough period. May we become Christ's faithful branches. May we bear much fruit in the coming days.

PRAYER:

> Lord Jesus, you are the vine and we are the branches. Prune everything which prevents me from being your faithful servant. In the light of your protecting and all encompassing love, may I graft others to you. Amen.

31

SCRIPTURE:

> "And then God said, 'Let the land produce living creatures according to their kinds, the livestock, the creatures that move along the ground, and the wild animals, each according to its kind.' And it was so. God made the wild animals, according to their kinds, the livestock according to their kinds, and all the creatures that move along the ground according to their kinds. And God saw that it was good" Genesis 1:24-25.

The fiftieth anniversary of Earth Day came and went without fanfare recently. Because of Covid-19 there were no parades or public gatherings marking the event. Nevertheless Earth Day entered greater consciousness when it was reported that smoggy Los Angeles registered clean air, the best in decades. Our atmosphere gives a shout out for reduced driving. In northern India, residents in cities and villages gaze at the snowy Himalayas, 125 miles away, a sight occluded for years by pollution. Perhaps wild animals 'celebrated' Earth Day by reclaiming areas from civilization's advance. There was a striking video of mountain lions bounding over an adobe wall to, well, chill out by someone's pool.

God created animals of all kinds for our benefit, domesticated and wild, because we would be impoverished without them. St. Francis of Assisi (1181-1226) founded the order which bears his name. Although he came from a wealthy family, he renounced riches and created a monastic community dedicated to a life of poverty, so that his followers could reach the impoverished. St. Francis is also the patron saint of animals. He prayed that he would be an instrument of God's love toward them. He preached sermons to them, recounting the ways God had blessed them. When St. Francis died, it was reported that larks swooped near his deathbed, warbling.

Like St. Francis I talk to my non-human brothers and sisters. Every morning I greet the sparrows who perch on my deck railing. At my condo complex, there is a lone Great Blue Heron who returns every Spring to fish our ponds. Each step it takes is deliberate and grace filled. I've seen it scrunch itself before its beak spears the water. With a single gulp a sunfish or bluegill becomes lunch. 'Well done,' I say. Whenever I spy it, I say a prayer, asking God to protect it. I worry, too, that it may get lonely. I've been told the bird is solitary by nature. No matter. If there were a matchmaking service for Great Blue Herons, I'd make a third party call!

There are dogs in our community. It seems I know their names better than their masked owners. And I have more to say to them. They're also much better listeners than their human counterparts. They keen to my baby talk, too, and make no judgments about my mental health status. They would understand that I am still in dialogue with my beloved mutt, Andy, (1989-2003). Early on a veterinarian explained that the puppy I had just adopted from the ASPCA would likely live no longer than a year given Andy's severe hip dysplasia. The doctor noted that increased weight would do my boy in. Andy overheard, and said, "Nuts" to any talk of an early exit!

We may be quarantined for a while, longer than we think, given yesterday's message from the CDC. I pray you have a non-human companion in your home, or, like me, your next door neighbor's. During this period we need all the support we can get. And our dogs, and cats; parakeets, and gerbils; horses, and turtles; are there, in their unique way, to provide it.

PRAYER:

> Lord, I thank you for surrounding me with animals
> with whom I can share affection and love. I am grateful
> for their forgiving and accepting natures. I thank you
> for wild animals in woods and fields, in the air and in
> the water, being who you call them to be. Let my mind
> inhabit the present as their minds do. May I exult in

every moment, as they do. May I be as free of future worry as they seem to be. May I embrace your loving creation more fully this day. Amen.

32
___

SCRIPTURE:

> "And not only that, but we also glory in our suffer-
> ings, knowing that suffering produces endurance, and
> endurance produces character, and character produces
> hope, and hope does not disappoint us, because God's
> love has been poured into our hearts through the Holy
> Spirit that has been given to us" Romans 5:3-5.

That Paul can glory in his suffering may seem absurd, given the
nature of the affliction we've witnessed, and the suffering we may
have endured these dark days. It would be easy to dismiss the apostle's statement were it not for the fact that he, too, suffered—the
stonings, beatings, floggings, along with shipwrecks and starvation.
All because of his evangelizing efforts. He catalogues the full extent
of his sorrows in 2 Corinthians 11:21-33; 12:1-10. Before he enu-
merates, however, he prefaces by writing: "We were under great
pressure, far beyond our ability to endure, so that we despaired of
life itself. Indeed, we felt we had been given the sentence of death"
(2 Corinthians 1:8-9). At this time do you feel as if you've been given
a psychological death sentence?

If Paul were sitting here today, he'd say that he can be trusted
because he's suffered more than we have. Comparing degrees
of affliction is a futile task. Not much fun! Paul notes that such
self-boasting sounds crazy to him! Nevertheless we are more apt
to heed the wisdom of a fellow sufferer than the individual who
has been spared whatever crown of thorns life delivers. The Apostle
helps us understand, and find meaning in our despair and terror
because he was immersed in those aspects himself.

Our suffering has purpose. It produces endurance, Paul writes.
Recently the President's medical task force noted that it is likely

Covid-19 may pursue us into the Fall. A dire prediction requiring us to hunker down and flat out endure. Through the power of the Holy Spirit, we can. God will give us the strength, the guts, the courage to outlast the Enemy. However long it takes, we will be conquerors.

Then Paul adds that endurance produces character. Think of it. Freud taught us that personality is formed during the Oedipal stage, at age five or six. Breaking with Freud, Object Relations theorists speculated that the decisive period was immediately after birth. Looking at his own life, the great theologian, Augustine (354-430) suggested that he 'came of age' as a young child when he first learned language. Social scientists today opine that character evolves, reaching its greatest potential in one's 20's when the prefrontal cortex of the brain fully develops.

Paul intimates that 'arrival' is based on perseverance in suffering. Thus we attain our characterological apex at any stage of life. We've seen it. It may be a child, or an elder. Or someone in between! They are our true heroes. And God gifts such people with an abiding hope which catastrophe can never extinguish. Be assured that God is shaping your character for his glory during this troubling period. Be assured that people will look at you, and see what it is possible to become.

PRAYER:

> Lord, I thank you for strengthening me. I believe that
> I can accomplish all things in and through you. May
> I sense your companionship, too, in moments when
> endurance wanes, and patience dwindles. Let me find
> new joy in daily tasks. In the fullness of your time, may
> I become more Christ-like to my very core. Amen.

33

"The beginning of wisdom is this: Get wisdom. Though it cost all you have, get understanding" Proverbs 4:7.

We are called to pay close attention whenever Scripture employs the imperative. The Hebrew prophets used the tense along with John the Baptist, and Jesus himself. God's mouthpieces, like Amos and Jeremiah, call for repentance here and now—in Israel, and Judah respectively—lest foreign powers destroy their nations. There's no time to defer or dither, they shouted. Immediate action was necessary. In the New Testament, John the Baptist proclaims, "The ax is already at the root of the trees, and every tree that does not bear good fruit will be cut down and thrown into the fire" (Matthew 3:10). Those who heard were baptized for forgiveness of their sins post-haste. Perhaps fright of the seemingly wild haired prophet, if nothing more, brought them to the Jordan river for a dunking.

After his forty day sojourn in the wilderness, Jesus began his public ministry announcing, "Repent, for the kingdom of heaven has come near" (Matthew 4:17). Note the imperative. Throughout his ministry Jesus taught the need for imminent, and radical change. Moving at a glacial pace is not what the Lord had in mind. We may understand the need to change, the necessity to puzzle out life's purpose, what the philosopher Sartre referred to as one's 'fundamental project.' But so often good times aid the procrastinator within. There's no rush, we say. We'll take care of soul searching next year; we'll examine the hidden, mysterious depths of our God-given beings next April. Or maybe the April after that. Heck, let's put it off for a half dozen Aprils, right after we complete our 2026 tax returns!

Covid-19 stokes the imperative. The death count may have

plateaued, but we cannot dismiss rising mortality rates in New York State, and our stricken country. God calls us to take our lives very seriously this moment. So we ask the questions we cannot postpone. 'What vocation must I pursue, and how do I prepare for it this very day?', a young person asks. The painter, or composer, the sculptor, or weaver questions his or her readiness to begin. He or she knows that inertia must be overcome instantly or the blank canvas will remain so for a lifetime. The frontline health care worker wrestles with job change—one which is safer, or one which involves greater risk. The choice can't be deferred. If you suffer from hypertension, obesity, or any predisposing factor, are you willing to abandon binge eating and non-exercise? Or will better health be palmed off as a future new year's resolution? Do we understand? Covid-19 accelerates decision making.

In his wonderfully succinct way, the author of Proverbs writes: "The beginning of wisdom is this: Get wisdom." Rilke wrote a poem in 1908 about an individual who gazes at the beauty of ancient Apollo's torso in a gallery. His poem ends, "You must change your life." The imperative drops like a bomb on the subject who seems content to contemplate a statue and, by extension, his navel. Take that first step. God will encourage and help.

PRAYER:

> Lord, help me to seek your wisdom this very moment. Let this day be one of reflection and action. Let Covid-19 provide the stimulus to understand myself more fully, and what you would have me do with this precious life you've given me. Lord, may I be the mouthpiece of your Good News. May I listen with Christ-like ears, and may I speak with divine approval, so that others may acquire your wisdom. Bless us all. And keep us safe. Amen.

34

SCRIPTURE:

> (Jesus said) "To what can I compare this generation?
> They are like children sitting in the marketplaces and
> calling out to others: 'We played the pipe for you, and
> you did not dance; we sang a dirge, and you did not
> mourn.' For John the Baptist came neither eating nor
> drinking, and they say, 'He has a demon.' The Son
> of Man came eating and drinking, and they say, 'He
> is a glutton and a drunkard, a friend of tax collectors
> and sinners.' But wisdom is proved right by her deeds"
> Matthew 11:16-19.

That American treasure, Billy Joel, wrote a song entitled, "The Angry Young Man". In it he sings, "I believe I've passed the age of consciousness and righteous rage/ I found that just surviving was a noble fight." Here! Here! Covid-19 shoves aside the inconsequential, as I lurch through one way supermarket aisles with my cart, like a drunken race car driver.

Recently I've started shopping at one of those supermarket warehouses where you can purchase a cannon ball sized jar of mayonnaise. Mine offers early morning concierge service for geezers like myself. I hand a written list to an employee who goes inside for me. The first time I tried it, the helpful attendee breached the 6 foot distancing rule by a good four feet, killing the purpose of the concierge service. I stuck my arm straight out to halt further advance, just like Charlton Heston's/Moses' outstretched arm against Pharaoh's army as they approached the Red Sea: "Thou shalt go no further," Heston bellowed. Or something like that. Whatever I said surprised the young woman, and she backed off. Being a guilt ridden Calvinist, I apologized profusely as she swiped my credit card. We left as friends, especially when another employee assisted, and discovered that my first and last names were the same as her husband's! "Lucky you", I said, and departed.

Once home, after every early morning odyssey, I spray each item with ammonia, as they clutter the flat-bed of my pick-up. I wait for the great outdoors to aid the window cleaner before wiping everything with microfiber cloths. I delay long enough so that ice cream turns soupy. What makes a basic task, like food shopping, so difficult is that no one in the government really knows how long Covid-19 adheres to, well, anything. Is it 'equal opportunity', or does it 'favor' plastic, or metal in its stay capacity? Several weeks ago it was announced by medical experts that the primary use of masks was to protect others from ourselves, the assumption is that we are the carriers. With the news that coughs have a firing range of twelve feet or more, and that the virus has hovering capacity as well, I believe that a mouth and nose covering may protect me as well as my neighbor.

Billy Joel speaks truth. Survival is a noble fight, particularly at this juncture. We need faith in our loving God to pull us through. If there is an upside, it is that survival draws attention away from trifles, like popularity assessments, among other things. Jesus addresses this issue in our text today. He notes that John's wonderfully ascetic, and simple life is defamed. His detractors state that such behavior constitutes demon possession. Then there's Jesus himself. He eats and drinks, and is slandered as a glutton and winebibber.

One can't win. Why try? Why try to prove our worth to the gossips, and mean spirits, those who may envy our commitment, and our compassion? Our Gospel lesson begs the question: In better times did we ruminate more than we should about whom we've displeased? Have we said to ourselves, 'How will I survive if my boss, friend, family member, or the entire Republican or Democratic party of Red Hook dislikes me? What will I do?'

You'll do just fine. Your heavenly Father loves you immeasurably. So does his lifegiving child, Jesus. Forget the gainsayers. During these plague ridden days, we don't have the energy to chew over negative opinions. Stick to the basics: Divine love for you. If you focus on that, you will not only survive; you will thrive.

PRAYER:

Lord, when it comes to affirmation, help me to gaze
vertically rather than horizontally. Thank you for
delivering me from the need to be liked by everyone.
Let me understand that you've blessed me with family
and friends who understand and support me no matter
what. Help me to understand the motives, and the
inherent unhappiness of my detractors. Give me the
power to care for them as well. I love you, Jesus. Amen.

35

> "Elijah was afraid and ran for his life. When he came
> to Beersheba in Judah, he left his servant there, while
> he himself went a day's journey into the wilderness. He
> came to a broom bush, sat down under it and prayed
> that he might die. 'I have had enough, Lord,' he said.
> 'Take my life. I am no better than my ancestors.' Then
> he fell asleep. All at once an angel touched him and said,
> 'Get up and eat.' He looked around, and there by his
> head was some bread baked over hot coals, and a jar of
> water. He ate and drank and then lay down again. The
> angel of the Lord came back to him a second time and
> touched him and said, 'Get up and eat for the journey
> is too much for you.' So he got up and ate and drank.
> Strengthened by that food, he traveled forty days and
> forty nights until he reached Horeb (Sinai) the mountain
> of God. There he went into a cave and spent the night.
> And the word of the Lord came to him, 'What are you
> doing here Elijah?' He replied, 'I have been very zealous
> for the Lord God Almighty. The Israelites have rejected
> your covenant, torn down your altars, and put your
> prophets to death by the sword. I am the only one left,
> and now they are trying to kill me too'" 1 Kings 19:3-10.

Elijah flees south because Queen Jezebel has sent her hit squad to murder him. The prophet manifests symptoms of Major Depressive Disorder. Sleeping too much or too little marks the illness. Elijah suffers from the former. An angel wakes him twice; we infer that he'd sleep forever, given the opportunity. Note, too, the angel tells him that he must eat, and supplies bread and water. Depressed people neglect eating or overeat. A rapid weight loss or gain is an indicator of depression. Food preparation seems overwhelming.

Isolation also signifies depression. Elijah leaves his servant at Beersheeba, and continues his journey of despair alone. Depression also globalizes negative thinking. Elijah tells God that Israel is rotten to the core—altars destroyed, the good prophets massacred. Elijah repeats the message a second time (vs. 14). Depressed folks will often parrot despair until it grooves the mind, scuttling rational capacity. Elijah's assessment is untrue. There are faithful prophets, and God's altar in Beersheba is still intact. Nevertheless Elijah cannot surface from the maelstrom.

Covid-19 contributes to depression's rise. Poet T.S. Eliot wrote, "April is the cruelest month." I'm unsure whether he had Major Depressive Disorder in mind, but he lit on a clinical truth. People so afflicted often think it will disappear once Spring arrives. Everything will be fine once he or she can get out, smell flowers, walk in green grass, and listen to birds. When one's mental state doesn't improve, the chasm deepens. Imagine then what our depressed neighbor experiences this April. Added to the profound let-down of a curative Spring is the 'blossoming' of Covid-19.

What to do? For some suicide becomes an attractive option. Suicide is the 'practical' extension of Major Depressive Disorder. One may have no control over coronavirus. But the individual can orchestrate self-annihilation. And that's one of the tricky aspects of suicide. People who plan to end their lives often seem less depressed than usual. They are because, for the first time, they control their destiny. And we, family and friends, are caught off guard by their sudden, sunny disposition.

Elijah had suicidal thoughts. "I have had enough, Lord," he said. "Take my life. I am no better than my dead ancestors." He's as good as dead, like his moldering relatives, although he still has a pulse and heartbeat. The threat of death dictated his heart cry. I think of our brave workers in the hospital. What does death's imminence do to them? I can't imagine. This month Covid-19 claimed the lives of two wonderful Reformed Church pastors—the best and brightest our denomination has ever produced. We attended New Brunswick

Seminary together. They were inspirations to our society, as well as the Reformed Church. Not only am I hollowed by their loss, but fear fills the vacuum; we were the same age. And both resided in upstate New York. If I'm scared, and live in relative safety, what kind of terror grips our health care workers? Again, I can't imagine.

Last Sunday young Dr. Lorna Breen ended her life at her family's home in Virginia. She headed the Allen Emergency Unit of New York Presbyterian Hospital. She contracted Covid-19, and survived. Instead of retreating, she continued to employ her considerable skills for the sake of her patients. She was a great leader as well as physician, we are told by those who worked with her. The best of the best. Her father asked that she be remembered as a hero. We won't forget her. I think of Elijah. Like Dr. Lorna, he was performing 'at the top of his game' on Mount Carmel, defeating the priests of Baal, as God consumed Elijah's offerings in a fiery display (1st Kings 18:16-46). At the height of his success he slid into depression, and suicidal ideation.

As Christians we are called to be mental health sleuths. Do you have a family member, a friend, a neighbor whose eating or sleeping habits have changed radically? Is there someone you know who no longer responds to your telephone calls or texts? When you talk to friend, does he or she express no interest in activities which always animated? Does he or she talk with flat affect? Do you know some-one who expresses the wish that God would end the individual's life? What about a loved one who trusts you enough to divulge a suicide plan? Don't dismiss it. Don't believe that the admission itself will prevent a suicide attempt. It won't.

We can be like Elijah's angel who commanded the prophet to awake, eat and drink. We must go further, however, in helping indi-viduals get the mental health and medical support they need.

PRAYER:

> Lord, make me be a messenger of your healing grace.
> Attune my ears, and mind to intuit when someone I
> know is in crisis. Help me to respond swiftly and lov-
> ingly as Jesus did for those in distress. Amen.

36

SCRIPTURE:

> "I thank my God every time I remember you. In all my
> prayers for all of you, I always pray with joy because
> of your partnership in the gospel from the first day
> until now, being confident in this that he who began a
> good work in you will carry it on to completion until
> the day of Jesus Christ...Now I want you to know,
> brothers and sisters, that what has happened to me
> has actually served to advance the gospel. As a result it
> has become clear throughout the whole palace guard,
> and to everyone else that I am in chains for Christ"
> Philippians 1:3-6; 12-13.

Paul's letter to the church he established in Philippi brims with joy.
The Apostle employs the word 16 times in this epistle, more than any
other letter. He addresses a congregation which accepted the Gospel,
and supported him. Paul was imprisoned in Ephesus, Caesarea, and
Rome. Although he gives no number, his statement in 2 Corinthians
11:23, implies that his 'slammer' residences exceeded three. Many
scholars believe that Philippians was written from Rome. Wherever
he was, imprisonment did not diminish gladness.

Perhaps we feel imprisoned by Covid-19. How can we experience
joy? Do what Paul did and write a letter to someone you love, or a
group you miss. How else? Let the missive specify how the addressee
has grown in faith. Those we love need our encouragement, need to
know, more specifically, that this pandemic has not stalled Christ's
wonderful work in that individual. Perhaps growth comes because
of the pandemic.

Paul also shows another way to experience joy in our in-home
imprisonment. Let folks see that our present state has not diminished

our capacity to help others encounter Christ. His imprisonment, "has served to advance the gospel" because he's become buddies with his jailers! In fact he may have converted some, knowing the Apostle's skill. Those we love from afar need to know, too, that we are flourishing, that we continue to be a positive force among those we encounter. We may not meet as many folks, it's true. But the quality of our interactions will more than compensate for the quantity of our pre-coronavirus encounters.

One of my buddies is a joyful Christian. Like most of us he, too, is under 'house arrest'. That hasn't slowed his evangelistic efforts. Recently a pizza delivery man rang his doorbell, and placed the order on the doormat. My friend tossed an envelope to the young man. My friend wore his clerical collar having just come from a videotaping session. The young man inquired about his vocation. They discussed Christianity for a good hour. In the meantime, the pizza had grown cold. The youth's spirits had been lifted. He took the moribund pie, and returned shortly with a piping hot replacement. Thanks be to God!

PRAYER:

> Lord help us to understand that you can use us for
> your glory. As your faithful servants, may we make
> the most of our 'in-house' time. May we be beacons of
> hope to those we encounter. Amen.

37

SCRIPTURE:

> "Live as children of the light (for the fruit of the light consists in all goodness, righteousness and truth) and find out what pleases the Lord. Have nothing to do with the fruitless deeds of darkness, but rather expose them" Ephesians 5: 8-11.

> "The wicked plot against the righteous and gnash their teeth at them; but the Lord laughs at the wicked for he knows their day is coming" Psalm 37:12-13.

Scams compound the terrors of coronavirus. An interesting business enterprise revealed itself this week: Landlords bartering rent for sex. Parking lot far ends turn into 'clinics' where quack Covid-19 tests, and cures are sold. Even a once prominent televangelist, who was sent to prison for scamming parishioners decades ago, has been promoting a Silver Solution as a viral antidote. Checks from the government are stolen, and robbers increasetheir chances by targeting the elderly particularly, pretending to be federal workers in need of additional information, like Social security and bank account numbers. Let's add those who corner the market on masks, and sanitizers, then sell them at an exponential mark-up, an endeavor which would have made P.T. Barnum blush.

For me one of the great strengths of the Christian religion is its realism about evil. Sin runs wide and deep. While Christians have always contended with the malign, it becomes more pronounced when it surfaces during national crises. We mistakenly believe that coronavirus, ipso facto, turns sinners into saints because of the common foe. My take is that snake oil salesmen rarely change. An epidemic simply emboldens. For the great majority, however, Covid-19 brings out the best. We witness inspirational accounts of charity and self-sacrifice. There are heroes who turn kitchens into food pantries; there are Kierkegaard's 'Knights of faith' whose belief leap is matched equally by their labors fifty or sixty hours a day, so it seems, meeting shut-in needs. Let's hear it for unpaid troubadours who serenade from street corners. What more can be said?

Nevertheless evil makes hay during times like these. What should we do? First, it is important to focus on the goodness we witness around us. Let's remain hopeful. That's not difficult when Christ-like acts abound. Second, we need not stew about those who take sinful advantage of the situation. We should get angry assuredly, that is the prophetic response. We would be remiss if we didn't. Nevertheless, as Paul admonishes, we should not "let the sun go down on our anger" (Ephesians 4:26). Let it go. It is important for our mental health. We have enough stressors. Don't add another. Third, have faith that God will deal with wickedness. I love this verse, "the Lord laughs for he knows their day is coming." Either in this life, or the life to come, evil people will get what they deserve. And they won't be laughing.

Finally, take action if you know of someone who is being victimized. Call law enforcement. Alert friends and neighbors. Confront scam artists wherever they lurk. Our New Testament reading calls us to "expose" "fruitless deeds". The Holy Spirit will help us with wisdom and power to accomplish the task.

PRAYER:

> Lord, help me to focus on the goodness of strangers I meet. Thank you for bringing out the best in humanity. Let me be one who finds inspiration in the loving deeds which daily come to my attention. Help me understand that I, too, am heroic. Thank you for supplying me with opportunities to make a difference. Lord, endow me with courage to confront evil whenever and wherever I witness it. Equip me with passion and compassion for the victimized. I pray in the name of my strong defender, Jesus Christ. Amen.

38

SCRIPTURE:

> "Paul and his companions traveled throughout the
> region of Phrygia and Galatia having been kept by the
> Holy Spirit from the preaching the word in the prov-
> ince of Asia. When they came to the border of Mysia,
> they tried to enter Bithynia, but the Spirit of Jesus
> would not allow them to. So they passed by Mysia
> and went down to Troas. During the night Paul had
> a vision of a man of Macedonia standing and begging
> him, 'Come over to Macedonia and help us.' After
> Paul had seen the vision we got ready at once to leave
> for Macedonia, concluding that God had called us to
> preach the gospel to them" Acts 16:6-10.

Paul attempted to evangelize the central and northern regions of
what we now call Turkey. In the Apostle's time the country had been
divided into various provinces, controlled by the Roman Empire.
Generally Paul's itinerary went in a north, north-easterly direction.
The only exception was Ephesus which broaches the Mediterranean
sea to the west. The Holy Spirit did not allow Paul to preach at the
most important city in Asia, although he would do so later. The
Holy Spirit also prevented the Apostle from preaching in the west-
ern part of Mysia, which bordered the Hellespont, and then, further
east, to the province of Bithynia which ran along the Black Sea.

Every right turn met a divine no. Thus Paul was forced to move
west, arriving in the port city of Troas where, in a vision, a man
from Macedonia begged him to shift his missionary efforts there.
Paul's European work would begin. Because of the Holy Spirit's
rerouting, the Apostle establishes churches down the eastern spine
of Greece, particularly in important cities like Philippi, Thessalonica,

and Corinth. In his second letter to the church at Corinth, Paul writes,"Now when I went to Troas to preach the Gospel of Christ and found that the Lord had opened a door for me...So I went on to Macedonia (2:12-13).

God provides open and closed doors. We may think we know exactly what our Lord would have us do. We're sure of our direction. Our spiritual GPS directs toward our personal Mysia, and Bithynia. Robert Frost's poem, 'The Road Not Taken' applies to others. Then God nixes our plans. We were certain of God's imprimatur on our life course. Then a door or two closes. We crane heavenward and ask, "What gives? I thought we shared the same roadmap."

The Covid-19 virus may afford more time to meditate on closed and open doors. The pandemic may 'confer' longer stretches for solitude which blesses in many ways, one of which is to better sense the Holy Spirit's subtle insistence on turning left rather than right. We may be saddened by the divine nudge in the opposite direction. That's understandable. Be assured that His direction will produce greater joy and purpose for us, and those we are called to serve. In Paul's case, I can understand that his brilliant, cosmopolitan mind may not have helped good country folk along the Black Sea. And if he had moved to Ephesus earlier, his work would not have been as effective as it was later.

Just so for us. God will direct us where we can be of greatest service, among those we can have the greatest impact. God equips us with special gifts for certain people with whom we can truly relate. Eventually Paul travels to Ephesus. A closed door opens for the Apostle. It may well be that our timing is not God's. So we never discount a closed door. It may simply be ajar.

On a plane bound for Tanzania, I sat next to a physician who was spending her vacation among children in a Nairobi hospital. She had fallen in love with Kenyans, and this would be her third tour. She was in her mid-50's. I asked her how long she had practiced. "I became a doctor four years ago", she smiled. "This was my dream, but raising children got in the way." She laughed. I told her my occupation. "So you believe in God's timing?" she asked. "I'm sitting next to a prime example," I replied.

PRAYER:

Lord, I thank you that I have been designed to follow your will wherever it leads. This day I thank you for closed doors. They direct my paths toward you as well those which open. Bless my faithful service. I am ready to be surprised by joy this day, this moment. Amen.

39

> "Yet we urge you, brothers and sisters, to do so more and more, and to make it your ambition to live a quiet life: You should mind your own business, and work with your hands, just as we told you, so that your daily life may win the respect of outsiders" 1 Thessalonians 4:10-11.

Covid-19 forces us to spend more time at home, which may have an upside when it comes to our understanding of neighborliness. Lately I spend leisure moments, talking to Sue next door, while her ancient auburn furred dog, Sky, bathes in the sun, more than willing to let 'grass grow beneath her paws.' Yesterday Sky lifted my deck door gate with her nose, inviting herself over for a nuzzle and a pat before she returned to Mommy and dinner. Just a friendly meet and greet; nothing lengthy, just enough smell time to assure that Uncle Bob is still Uncle Bob.

I discover the joys of small talk among those who pass by my condo. A wave, a 'How are you?' asked from an appropriate distance; discussion about the upcoming weather; the best restaurant for curbside pick-up. Recently a couple asked me to supply information how best to access food from a superstore without entering, an answer I supplied happily. I have lived in this complex for three years, and a number of people know my vocation. No one really cares, or perhaps cares little. Disused are titles. The only thing I know about a neighborly retired physician is that he likes a particular sushi restaurant, and longs for the day it reopens. I bet if I asked about his medical specialty he'd ignore me.

As Paul enjoins, I live quietly—no indoor mosh pitting, no Bacchanals, no hammering electrified guitar strings in the middle of the night. Just a grateful submersion into everyday patter. I mind my own business which is not difficult in our wonderfully staid community. I work with my hands, at least to cook, and write. Just don't ask me to screw in a lightbulb! Perhaps being a faithful Christian is to be a good neighbor without necessarily calling attention to our faith, or ourselves. People know who we serve without our mentioning. They'll intuit our faith by the way we insert hope unobtrusively into 'How's the weather?' conversation.

PRAYER:

> Lord, make me an instrument of your hope. Allow me to be a quiet presence in my community. Make me the yeast which ever so subtly leavens the loaf of fellowship in my neighborhood. May I find your joy in losing myself in the daily interests and cares of those where you have placed me. Equip me be to be your faithful servant this day. Amen.

40

SCRIPTURE:

> "The Lord said to Abram, 'Go from your country, your people and your father's household to the land I will show you. I will make you into a great nation, and I will bless you; I will make your name great, and you will be a blessing...and all peoples on earth will be blessed through you.' So Abram went, as the Lord had told him; and Lot went with him. Abram was 75 years old when he set out from Harran, and they set out for the land of Canaan, and they arrived there. Abram traveled through the land as far as the site of the great tree of Moreh at Shechem...From there he went on toward the hills east of Bethel and pitched his tent with Bethel on the west and Ai on the east. There he built an altar to the Lord and called on the name of the Lord. Then Abram set out and continued toward the Negev" Genesis: 12:1-9.

Through Abram God established His holy nation. Jesus' royal lineage begins with this great man of faith (Matthew 1:1). At age 75 he leaves the comforts of Harran, and heads south with his family, trusting God's call. He obeys immediately, without questioning. No stall, or dither on his part. Note, too, his adventure begins as a geezer, a time when he was collecting Social Security, perfecting his putting technique at the Harran Country Club; writing an advice column for seniors; and developing a retirement community: 'Happy Harran Estates' where the clubhouse is well appointed with an indoor gym, jacuzzi and sauna.

What dreams did the old boy abandon? For us seniors, God's press may come at odd times. It may begin at 75, or 80—as with

Moses—or whatever age God conscripts us to embark on journeys we could not imagine even in our younger years. Age is no barrier. We are never too old to change directions, to move from present day comfort into God's strange, yet wonderfully stunning future.

Our journey may not be geographic. It probably isn't what with moving companies not moving folks at this juncture. We are called to make mind strides, caravanning across soul expanse, bringing others, as did Abram. The disorienting journey begins when the introvert phones non-stop to see how he or she can help others. It starts when the inveterate bank or stock account riffler lays aside paper, and handles cloth to make face masks. God's call initiates when the frazzled health care worker finds peace in something new and seemingly out of character: Simply sitting in meditation, and prayer, discovering that he or she draws others by repose modeling.

Abram is continually on the move in the narrative. He lands in Canaan, but the Almighty prods him further, so that he leaves foreign civilization for what? The Negev, the wilderness, no man's land. Lots of sand and little water; frangible rock formations where skinks dart, and vipers nest. In the sky kestrels and vultures soar above the little caravan, the latter casting more than a disinterested eye on the wearied band. God gives Abram and his family no compass, or road map. Absent are welcome centers and the incandescent blink of a faulty Wilderness Hilton sign to help them orient. Nothing. The author of Hebrews writes: "By faith Abraham, when called to go to a place he would later receive as his inheritance, obeyed and went out not knowing where he was going"(11:8). Amen to that.

That's us. Covid-19 is a disorienting wilderness. Sometimes we haven't a clue where we're headed psychologically. Although our environment may not have changed, we may feel as if we reside in a strange, foreboding land. The ways we navigated a pre-coronavirus world seem useless now. Nevertheless, like Abraham we walk by faith. When other props fall by the wayside, sheer belief in God's call drives us. May we embrace His future this day.

Lord, let me be your faithful pilgrim. I'll follow wherever you lead. I look forward to what awaits. Use me to guide others through their wildernesses. Amen.

41

> "Jesus said, 'A man was going down from Jerusalem to Jericho, when he was attacked by robbers. They stripped him of his clothes, beat him and went away, leaving him half dead. A priest happened to be going down the same road, and when he saw the man he passed by on the other side. So, too, a Levite, when he came to the place and saw him, passed by on the other side. But a Samaritan, as he traveled, came where the man was; and when he saw him, he took pity on him. He went to him and bandaged his wounds, pouring on oil and wine. Then he put the man on his own donkey, brought him to an inn and took care of him. The next day he took out two denarii and gave them to the innkeeper. 'Look after him,' he said, 'and when I return, I will reimburse you for any extra expense you may have.' Which of these three do you think was a neighbor to the man who fell into the hands of robbers?' The expert in the law replied, 'The one who had mercy on him.' Jesus told him, 'Go and do likewise'"
> Luke 10:30-37.

Jews hated Samaritans. They were considered half breeds, and prevented from entering the Temple in Jerusalem. One would jaywalk to avoid encounter. More than seven hundred years before Jesus' parable, Samaria, Israel's capital, was leveled by an Assyrian army. Assyria was the greatest world power at that time. Their method of subjugation involved marching intelligentsia to one of their cities hundreds of miles east. In the British museum one can observe stone friezes of Israel's captivity. The Jewish prisoners were hooked in the nose, an effective way of thwarting escape as they plodded eastward. Assyria completed its work by flooding the conquered area with non-Jews, knowing that interbreeding would dilute religion fueled rebellion. Assyria did its work well. There were no revolts, and no worry about alliances with Jews. In Jesus' day Samaritans were considered sub-human.

No wonder the parable scandalized. That a Samaritan would aid a Jew seemed absurd. Laughable in fact. Jesus told the tale to illustrate the incongruence of mercy and racism. Perhaps coronavirus upends invidious racial and ethnic stereotyping or at least dampens the urge. Imagine someone you know who holds discriminatory views. Make the individual the victim in Jesus' parable. Your choice for gender.

Your neighbor is not robbed literally. But life is being stolen as lungs struggle for air; note the bug-eyed stare glued to the monitor. What do the rhythmic blips, coming from somewhere, and the surrounding tubal ganglia portend? Now he or she discovers that the looming face—blurred by a plate glass thick plastic shield—is someone whose race is different. Let's say the visage is that of a Chinese physician. Since there has been a lot of Asian bashing lately, imagine your neighbor is quite fond of placard carrying. Nothing better to do on a bright, sunny Saturday than yell at 'foreigners' to return to China—and take the virus with them. And then. Our patient survives. He waits to cross the street, placard free. He spots a familiar face from the ICU. What does he or she do? We have a hunch.

My father fought in World War 2 and Korea. In the former his platoon found itself behind enemy lines in Belgium. A German officer was captured. The captain said to my father, "Lieutenant Gram, go into the woods and lose him." 'Lose' was euphemistic for execution. My father was in Army intelligence, so he knew the terrain. He found a nearby monastery, knocked on the door, and said to the monk who answered, "He's yours now." My aunt told this story after Dad had passed. Men and women of that generation were too humble to boast. My father would never have viewed himself as a Good Samaritan. To that German officer, he certainly was.

PRAYER:

Lord, I pray that hearts and minds will be changed.
May this pandemic unite us more closely as a nation,
so that that what we have in common far outweighs
our differences. Bless us and keep us this day. Amen.

42

"There was a man who had two sons. The younger one said to his father, 'Father, give me my share of the estate.' So he divided his property between them. Not long after that, the younger son got together all he had, set off for a distant country and there squandered his wealth in wild living. After he had spent everything, there was a severe famine in that whole country, and he began to be in need. So he went and hired himself out to a citizen of that country, who sent him to his fields to feed pigs. He longed to fill his stomach with the pods that the pigs were eating, but no one gave him anything. When he came to his senses, he said, 'How many of my father's hired servants have food to spare, and here I am starving to death! I will set out and go back to my father and say to him: 'Father, I have sinned against heaven and against you. I am no longer worthy to be called your son; make me like one of your hired servants.' So he got up and went to his father. But while he was still a long way off, his father saw him and was filled with compassion for him; he ran to his son, threw his arms around him and kissed him" Luke 15:11-20.

This is the 'front half' of Jesus' most famous parable. Later commentators dubbed it the story of the 'Prodigal Son', or the 'Loving Father'. Both titles fit. If one reads further, we encounter the elder son who accuses his father of unseemly if not downright unethical behavior by his embrace of his younger sibling. He resents his brother, and accuses him of consorting with prostitutes, a charge which 'wild living' may or may not connote. It's easy to infer that he indicts his 'permissive' father as well as his miscreant brother. If we shift emphasis to the elder brother, we might entitle Jesus' words as the 'Parable of the Ungrateful Brother'.

In this pandemic era, I would entitle it: 'The Parable of the Brokenhearted Parent.' Covid-19 sharpens the lineament of the father-son relationship. Put yourself in the father's or parent's position. You have a child who has hurt you deeply. He or she has broken the relationship and your heart. You are separated by miles, and, with quarantines in place, there is little hope of a geographical about face even if your child sought it. Then there is the threat that your son or daughter might not return because he or she has contracted the viral terror. Or, perhaps, you're the feverish one who packs a small suitcase for the nearest Emergency Room. Either way, the thought of permanent separation is hard to bear. In fact it is impossible to bear.

Corona virus raises the stakes, doesn't it? Suddenly it becomes very clear that whatever the sin, whatever the affront doesn't matter a lick when we sight our beloved. In fact the concept of forgiveness is irrelevant, as if we would cleave to our prodigal—neck vein to neck vein—only if he or she repented. In the parable the father lavishes kisses before the boy can say anything. Can we imagine Dad's bearhug, constricting the young man so that he cannot croak an 'I'm sorry', let alone the elaborate confession. The Prodigal does confess, but it is irrelevant to Dad; his mind races ahead, what with booking the child's favorite rock band ASAP; making sure there is a spread for vegetarians as well as the gaggle of lamb eaters who will shortly descend. Then there's the champagne to order, and 'Welcome Home' banners to be draped on the barn walls. So much to do, but time worries vanish, and the father's mind rotates on embracing his beloved until his arms ache, until time condenses to such a degree that the hug more than compensates for the months or years of separation.

May we anticipate the joys of reunion with someone with whom we are estranged. It may be a child. It may be a spouse or a friend, a lover or sibling. Believe that Jesus manages a variety of reconciliations during this sad time. That's why he told this marvelous parable. That we might have great hope.

PRAYER:

Lord, you know my heart breaks for a relationship which has been sundered. I pray for its restoration. Despite social distancing, may my beloved experience my embrace by the loving words I speak, by the letters I write, by my laughter, and my inexpressible joy he or she sees on Facebook, or Zoom, or whatever channel I employ. May your love for me radiate in the love I share for the returning prodigal. Amen.

43

SCRIPTURE:

> "When the Lord was about to take Elijah up to heaven in a whirlwind, Elijah and Elisha were on their way from Gilgal. Elijah said to Elisha, 'Stay here; the Lord has sent me to Bethel.' But Elisha said, 'As surely as the Lord lives and as you live, I will not leave you.' So they went down to Bethel. The company of the prophets at Bethel came out to Elisha and asked, 'Do you know that the Lord is going to take your m aster from you today?' 'Yes, I know,' Elisha replied, 'so be quiet.' Then Elijah said to him, 'Stay here Elisha; the Lord has sent me to Jericho.' And Elisha replied, 'As surely as the Lord lives and as you live, I will not leave you.' So they went to Jericho. The company of the prophets at Jericho went up to Elisha and asked him, 'Do you know that the Lord is going to take your master from you today?' 'Yes I know,' he replied, 'so be quiet.' Then Elijah said to him, 'Stay here for the Lord has sent me to the Jordan.' And Elisha replied, 'As surely as the Lord lives, and as you live, I will not leave you.' So the two of them walked on…As they were walking along and talking together, suddenly a chariot of fire and horses of fire appeared and separated the two of them, and Elijah went up to heaven in a whirlwind. Elisha saw this and cried out, 'My father! My father!…Then Elisha saw him no more. Then he took hold of his garment and tore it in two" 2 Kings 2:1-6; 11-12.

The pandemic certainly sharpens awareness of death, and grieving. Today's text explores the nature of mourning. A popular misconception is that we can gear up for a loved one's passing if we know well in advance the prognosis and its course. We can't. Believe me. Clinically 'anticipatory grief' is the term used for death prepping. Anticipatory grieving may help while a terminally ill loved one still lives. But it can't mitigate our plunge to sorrow's nadir once death arrives. Nor would we want it. If we have loved deeply we will grieve deeply. That's the price we pay for being self-giving, compassionate human beings. Better that than its opposite, a life skirting relational depth. 'Better to have loved and lost, than to have never loved at all.' True but trite. The aphorism rings hollow, given the soundings of a maimed soul.

Elisha is Elijah's spiritual son, and will soon acquire the gifts of his teacher and spiritual father. He is certainly well aware of his teacher's end. His mentor has mentioned it. If for a moment Elisha forgets, those pesky prophets in various locations will remind. Is Elisha prepared? Apparently not. When Elijah ascends to heaven in a fiery chariot, Elisha rips his robe in two, a sign of despair. Words cannot fill the sorrowing vacuum. Even if he understood the concept, Elisha would admit he is far afield from anticipatory grief. The concept disappears beneath the renting tunic.

Note, too, that Elisha gazes at Elijah's upward flight. There's no doubt where the great prophet is headed. A smiling heaven awaits. Yet Elisha still grieves. Some believe that mourning signals a lack of faith. The argument goes like this: 'If your loved one is going to a better place, shouldn't you be happy?' 'Well, no', we might respond. 'I'm glad for him or her, but not for me as I sit transfixed before the empty space at the dinner table, where I've set fork, knife and spoon for decades. And this persistent forgetfulness impels me to prepare a place setting, over and over, expecting what?' Well his or her reappearance, that's what.' We keen for a familiar footfall as he or she descends the stairs, readying for dinner. Poet Emily Dickinson once wrote: "I measure every grief I meet/ With narrow probing eyes—I wonder if it weighs like Mine/Or has an Easier size." If we have loved deeply, then Emily's size fits all, thank goodness.

Jesus said, "Blessed are those who mourn for they shall be comforted" (Matthew 5:4). That's our hope. If we mourn deeply—no holding back, no stiff upper lip here in the land of loss— Christ will fill us with his love. That will carry us. For Elisha mourning moves to prophetic service where he duplicates his master's miracles in Elijah's honor. May we, too, honor our deceased by incorporating their lives of faith, and action into our own.

PRAYER:

> Heavenly Father, bring balm and healing to my
> wounded self. I have been halved, and wonder whether
> I'll ever be whole. Is there repair? Use my grief to
> honor my loved one, and to be of service to others who
> mourn. Work a miracle in my wounding this very day,
> this very moment. Amen.

44

SCRIPTURE:

> "Now a man named Lazarus was sick. He was from
> Bethany, the village of Mary and her sister Martha...So
> the sisters sent word to Jesus, 'Lord, the one you love
> is sick.' When he heard this, Jesus said, 'This sickness
> will not end in death. No, it is for God's glory, so that
> God's Son may be glorified through it.' Now Jesus
> loved Martha and her sister and Lazarus. So when he
> heard that Lazarus was sick, he stayed where he was
> for two more days, and then he said to his disciples,
> 'Let us go back to Judea.'...On his arrival, Jesus found
> that Lazarus had already been in the tomb for four
> days...When Martha heard that Jesus was coming,
> she went out to meet him, but Mary stayed at home.
> 'Lord,' Martha said to Jesus, 'if you had been here, my
> brother would not have died. But I know that even
> now God will give you whatever you ask.' Jesus said to
> her, 'Your brother will rise again.'" John 11:1-7; 17-22.

Initially the delay seems strange, and out of character. Lazarus boarders on death, and Jesus dallies for two extra days. Lazarus' sister, Martha, believes her brother could have been cured if the Galilean miracle worker had arrived on time. What would her response have been had she known that Christ dithered as her brother died. Perhaps anger would have laced her despair. Lazarus' resurrection hinged on Jesus' delay. Arriving on time meant a sick man's cure. Jesus would have been proclaimed a miracle worker, one of many at that time. Arriving late allowed messianic hailing, the result of Lazarus' full bodied resuscitation— emphasized by Martha's blunt remark about stench from the tomb.

Delays may be important in our pandemic age. Of course we need to act swiftly. That's Jesus' method. Taking a loved one to the emergency room; piling groceries into your car when you discover by chance that a neighbor's cupboard is bare. Speed is essential in the emergency rooms of countless hospitals, and ambulance rides in the middle of the night. Nevertheless sometimes waiting, as Jesus did, allows circumstances to develop. Last February, before the outbreak, a young couple asked me to perform their wedding in June. Two weeks ago the prospective bride called to announce the wedding was cancelled. I asked whether she planned to reschedule once the virus ends? "No," she answered. "This sounds crazy, Pastor. But I think what's going on outside gave me time to think. I don't want to marry him ever." Poor guy! The nuptials done in by a coronavirus delay. Sufficient time allows the altar bound to say, 'I don't' rather than 'I do.'

I've witnessed other examples. Being cooped up with his parents during this quarantine allowed a friend's son to apply to a school which trains forest rangers. Time at home made him realize that a desk job is exactly what he didn't want. Although the subject matter of his indoor vocation still held interest, it was insufficient to detour his new 'tree hugging' path. Then there's an elderly woman in my former congregation who planned on having a picnic last week on one of those rare warm days. She and her friend had both self-quarantined, and felt safe to be together. They would wear masks, of course. My parishioner cancelled at the last minute because she lost her cell phone, and felt uncomfortable without it. They rescheduled. Two days later her friend called to say that she had tested positive for the virus. Thank goodness for a missing cellphone—my parishioner discovered it in the freezer of all places. Once again God is thanked for an 'unintended' delay.

Jesus' deferral confirmed his messianic status. What did it mean for Lazarus? I wonder whether life was never more precious than when he stepped from the tomb; it would have been far more meaningful than if he left a sickbed. Perhaps Lazarus really saw the familiar with repristinated eyes. His beautiful sisters. The milling sheep and goats edging toward him with 'Welcome Back' bleats. Stunned neighbors emptying pantries so that the town square soon filled with partying whoops, a regular hoe down, with a fiddler and Texas two stepping to boot! Even Lazarus' first footfalls on familiar earth must have seemed as if he treaded, like Moses before the burning bush, on holy ground.

Suppose God's delays are so finely calibrated that your life is forever altered? In a former congregation, my parishioner was a high powered lawyer in Manhattan. Rumor had it that ethics shaving was his forte. He loved his wife which meant that he allowed her to drag him by the ear to church every Sunday. It was the last place he wanted to be. One summer he skippered a small boat somewhere off the Florida coast. A storm arose and he capsized. Food and water were not tied; he realized there was no chance of survival if rescue was delayed. He tried to wave down a passing boat but it didn't spot him. Nor did a second.

On the third day a Coast guard vessel pulled him to the deck. After he was given a physical exam, and wolfed down sandwiches and water, the captain apologized that he had to endure three days in the ocean. The lawyer's reply must have stunned him. My parishioner said, "Your timing was perfect. If you had discovered me a day or two later I'd probably be dead. Any earlier, and I wouldn't have changed." The captain may not have understood, but his wife, and I did. Figuratively, like Lazarus, he had risen from the dead. His business practices changed for the better. He tithed. And now it was he who dragged his wife to church, Sunday after Sunday! God's perfectly timed delay yielded optimum results!

PRAYER:

> Lord, help me understand that delays are part of your plan for my growth. Let me view Covid-19 as an avenue you use to reorder my projects and altar my priorities. Resurrect me to new understandings of what you would have me be, and what you would have me do. Amen.

45

> "When they came, he looked on Eliab and thought, 'Surely the Lord's anointed is now before the Lord.' But the Lord said to Samuel, 'Do not look on his appearance or the height of his stature, because I have rejected him; for the Lord does not see as mortals see; they look on the outward appearance, but the Lord looks on the heart" 1 Samuel 16:6-7.

In our text God calls the prophet Samuel to anoint a new king. Eliab may have looked the part, but God dismisses him. Beauty resides in the heart rather than in outward appearance. That's the message. Not that Scripture takes no notice of physical beauty. Several verses later God chooses a shepherd boy named David. Eliab's youngest brother is described in glowing terms: "Now he was ruddy, and had beautiful eyes, and was handsome" (vs. 16). The description is repeated before David challenges Goliath (17:42). The writer of 2 Samuel absolutely gushes over King David's son: "Now in all Israel there was no one to be praised so much for his beauty as Absalom; from the sole of his foot to the crown of his head there was no blemish in him. When he cut the hair of his head...he weighed the hair of his head, two hundred shekels by the king's weight" (14:25-26). No doubt Absalom would be pushing shampoo or skin rejuvenators in our day and age.

The Bible also limns the physical attributes of women. Sarah, Rebekah, Bathsheba, and Tamar are described as beautiful in appearance. What can we say about the Song of Songs? The entire book is a paean to feminine beauty; we're talking about outward looks here, writ rather graphically, enough for prudes to blush, and theologians to allegorize. Is this book in Scripture? Really?

It is interesting then, that we find no physical description of Jesus in the New Testament. Indeed the most important person in Scripture is faceless. Nevertheless artists throughout the centuries have tried to capture the mystery of his appearance. The earliest church, adhering to the letter of the 2nd Commandment, refused to paint Christ. A good Jew dared not "make a graven image" of God; a good Christian, owing to his Jewish background, dared not represent God's full manifestation in Christ. The stricture receded as the faith moved out into the Mediterranean world.

By the third century Jesus was depicted in catacombs, Roman sewers, and Christian meeting houses above ground. Youthful, curly haired, and beardless, he became the handsome Roman boy-man. By the middle of the Fourth Century, Jesus' face, chiseled on sarcophagi, portrayed the regal Christ. The earthy Galilean is subsumed. Jesus gained in size as the Byzantine era progressed, and, by the 12th Century, he had been enthroned on the apses and walls of churches and cathedrals. Solemn, otherworldly, and monumental, Jesus' humanity disappears in heavenly aura.

It was not until the Florentine artist Giotto (1267-1337), that the splendor of the Byzantine, yielded to Jesus' humanity. In his fresco, 'The Betrayal', Jesus stands nose-to-nose with his accuser, Judas. A mob surrounds them. Jesus is a man—there is a new found realism. Compared to the others in the scene, however, he is a perfect man. The handsome angularity of his face, rather than his halo, emphasizes his divinity. With the flowering of the Italian Renaissance, painters like Michelangelo took Giotto's Jesus, and turned him into an Olympian. The fair face now combines with striated muscles.

Handsome Jesus has been with us ever since. Just look at all the Jesus' movies and musicals which have been produced this century and the last. In Nicolas Ray's 1961 production, 'King of Kings', blonde, haired blue eyed Jeffrey Hunter played the starring role. He performed credibly, but was unkindly dubbed by one reviewer as the 'Teen-age Surfer Jesus'. Amen to that in terms of looks. Perhaps we picture Jesus throughout history the way we look at ourselves. We make him one of us, or at least a figure we'd like to be.

Given Covid-19 how would we paint Jesus? Would his face be

hidden behind a face mask? Would the eyes be rheumy from over-work in a critical care unit? Would his cheeks be tear smudged, watching a favorite nursing home patient die? Would the pockets beneath his eyes puff? Would threading crows-feet deepen into grooves, the result of worry as much as genes? Would he look disheveled because his front line duties afford no time to shower and shave? Would his eyes close, and face furrow as a loved one is dashed off on a gurney from the Emergency Room into the milling, overwrought bowels of a hospital? What would his face betray having been told a loved one was dying, and that he could not see, let alone touch, his dearest companion?

What would Jesus look like in this present pandemic? We may have a clue. This day we have done our best for others. We have cared for them, we have risked for them, we have communicated faithfully again and again, so that we are careworn as the day ends. Then we arrive at the bathroom before retiring. And gaze in the mirror. For an instant we glimpse a face, other than our own.

PRAYER:

> Dear Lord, help me to be a faithful companion this
> day for all who need your compassion. May I choose
> my words carefully. May my actions reflect love for
> all who are afflicted. In my service, may they see the
> face of the One I love, the One I try faithfully to serve.
> Amen.

46

> "When they finished breakfast, Jesus said to Simon
> Peter, 'Simon son of John, do you love me more than
> these?' He said to him, 'Yes, Lord; you know that I
> love you.' Jesus said to him, 'Feed my lambs.' A second
> time he said to him, 'Simon, son of John, do you love
> me?' He said to him, 'Yes, Lord; you know that I love
> you.' Jesus said, 'Tend my sheep.' He said to him a
> third time, 'Simon, son of John, do you love me?' Peter
> felt hurt because he said to him the third time, 'Do you
> love me?' And he said to him, 'Lord, you know every-
> thing; you know that I love you.' Jesus said to him,
> 'Feed my sheep'" John 21:15-17.

Jesus understood the difficulty of preaching to a crowd of empty stomachs. So his Good News got even better with fish grease glossing the lips of his followers, their wetted thumbs picking up bread crumbs from robes. Good News can't be good unless feeding goes along with teaching, a message which reverberates throughout our day as Covid-19 disrupts food chains throughout the world. Jesus noted that we see him whenever we give food and drink as well as comfort to the sick, the naked, the imprisoned, and the stranger (Matthew 25:35-45).

Feeding the world may well be our fundamental task. I'm so proud of St. John's food pantry. Churches in the area are well stocked, then emptied quickly as food shortage grows. Minus a pantry, congregations deliver homecooked meals to shut-ins. Several days ago I entered our fellowship hall before the latest run on food began. No one was around. I gazed at cans and packaged goods rising from tables and kitchen work areas like stalagmites. There's an aesthetic to these spires. Some parishioners have taken videos. Can we say that there is beauty in feeding the hungry.

Food is important in our present text. Before Jesus questions Peter, he prepares breakfast for the disciples after their hourly grind on the Sea of Galilee. Thus the post as well as the pre-resurrection Christ sets about feeding his closest friends. Jesus calls Peter to assume the role after Jesus ascends. So the chef's hat is passed to the primary disciple. Get the spatulas ready, boys. There are lots of mouths to feed. Let me digress briefly to note that Peter's three fold affirmation of love represents the Gospel writer's balancing Peter's restoration with his betrayal. After Jesus' arrest, during his trial, Peter denied knowing Jesus three times, as the Lord predicted. At one point he even curses him when the woman accuser persists in her accusation. Instead of a threefold denial, Peter affirms his love for his Savior three times. What a lovely touch.

Let me return to the word 'feeding'. Jesus brings it up twice in our story, and often we take it figuratively. We are called to feed others with the good news of the Gospel. We feed them by what we teach, and preach. They ingest our wise counsel, and consoling words. They are sated because we've explained the details of filing for unemployment insurance, and Medicaid. Essentially 'feeding' is the metaphor for good news talking.

In light of Covid-19 let me view the word iterally, and personalize. Feeding may mean spooning soup into the mouth of a sick child, or mother with whom you are quarantined. Feeding may involve cutting up unintended al dente broccoli for a loved one whose throat is still raw from hospital intubation. Feeding is steadying the hand of a spouse whose Parkinson's Disease has 'acted up' during the pandemic; your hand wraps tighter around his or hers as the jittering spoon creases the lips. Feeding may be saying to your addled homebound grandparent that you are not leaving the room until the jaw unclenches and the medicine is swallowed.

'Sheep', too, is an apt metaphor in this context. You may be sequestered with those who are sick, those who would be lost the moment they stepped foot out the front door. That's why you keep it double bolted. God calls you to be a shepherd which means dexterity with a fork and spoon rather than a staff. Who are the sheep who need the ongoing support and love you supply? Who are those who would starve without your day to day cooking and coaxing?

I met Brother Stan at a monastery in southern New York. Back in the early 70's I was working on a Master's Thesis about Christians and Jews helping one another in history's greatest charnel house, Auschwitz. Brother Stan resided in a Capuchin monastery in Krakow, Poland when World War 2 erupted. The monastery quickly became an underground railroad for Jews fleeing Nazi persecution. Periodically the Gestapo would inspect it, fearing the brothers were in cahoots with refugees. They were. One day the Gestapo paid a surprise visit, and discovered that the number of brothers had increased fourfold. Thus Brother Stan and his Capuchin confreres, as well as the newly minted Jewish 'monks', were taken in a cattle car to Auschwitz, 60 miles away.

Brother Stan survived the extermination camp. He was imprisoned there for three and a half years, one of the few who defied the calculus of terribly shortened lives. During that period he hollowed out the heel of his boot, and kneaded flat wafers from moldy bread scraps. Then he trudged through the gray mud, surrounding the camp. Prisoners tried to escape; few did. Even if they were able to struggle through the gummy clay, they'd have to scrabble up the electrified barbed wire fence—an impossibility. For some it was better to die in the 'open' than in lice filled barracks. Indeed escape was not on their minds. Brother Stan followed them. He approached those rooted in mud. He said, "Do you know that God loves you?" Often prisoners were too weak to speak. But they nodded. Then they opened their mouths and Brother Stan placed his homespun Host on their tongues; sometimes they needed his help to chew. He moved their jaws up and down. Then he prayed for them.

He was not trying to make fellow sufferers good Roman Catholics. He simply wanted them to know that if Jesus were there, he'd be feeding them. "Give us this day our daily bread", the Master prayed. I have doubts if I am heaven bound. I believe my friend, Brother Stan, is there unquestionably. My fondest hope is that there are great stewpots in the elysian realm. If I am invited, I will request a seat next to him. One of our arms each will be tied behind our backs. We'll be given a wooden ladle each, long enough to reach the pot, but too long to bring it to our mouths. The ladles will be just the right length to feed one another. Roast beef or lamb, my dear brother?

PRAYER:

> Lord I thank you for supplying my basic needs. Help me to believe that you will always provide. In that confidence help me to feed the lost sheep of your world. Amen.

47

SCRIPTURE:

"Now on that same day two of them were going to a village called Emmaus, about seven miles from Jerusalem and talking with each other about all these things that had happened. While they were talking and discussing, Jesus himself came near and went with them, but their eyes were kept from recognizing him. And he said to them, 'What are you discussing with each other while you walk along?' They stood still, looking sad. 'Are you the only stranger in Jerusalem who does not know the things that have taken place in these days?'...As they came to the village to which they were going, he walked ahead as if he were going on. But they urged him strongly, saying, 'Stay with us because it is almost evening and the day is now nearly over.' So he went in to stay with him. When he was at the table with them, he took bread, blessed and broke it, and gave it to them. Then their eyes were open, and they recognized him; and he vanished from their sight" Luke 24:13-28; 28-31.

The Emmaus story redivivus. I've abbreviated the text slightly from my first entry because I want to focus on the unseen as well as seen messiah. Jesus enters as a stranger, then becomes their dearest friend once more. The puzzle continues as the bread breaker becomes the Vanisher who departs before the lemon tarts and a lovely port can draw the evening to a close. He disappears faster than a magician's assistant without so much as a by-your-leave—into the resolute darkness, leaving the disciples confused at the very least. Did possible wine chugging on the road help conjure a third companion?

Or did grief alone bollix their thinking? Or were they hallucinating for reasons unknown? Or is the Master a trickster, a game player, 'messing with our heads' as young people say? The worst day of their lives followed by the best day, followed by the worst day in the span of hours.

Suppose his presence and disappearance represent two poles, the dialectic which strengthens faith. At times we need signs of Christ's immanence. Someone comes into our lives at the moment we need that person most. Maybe you arrive at the supermarket wrapped in your face mask, worrying that you might get infected by a host of other harried shoppers. And surprisingly, miraculously, no one is there, save you and the cashier, and one or two cart pushers, thumping cantaloupe at one end of the store, while you squint at milk expiration dates on the other. You've been told by someone with whom you're quarantined that he or she really loves you, more than ever. Suddenly you must retool your thinking because you've always believed—isn't it in Scripture?—that absence alone makes the heart grow fonder, and that sequestering will kill any relationship.

Let's say the physicians and nurses are removing lifesaving equipment from your spouse. That's the rumor, but there is no indication he or she has been taken to a less intensive ward. You knew how grave his situation is. Panicking you race to the nearest funeral director, trying to figure whether a wood or metal casket is more representative of your spouse's wishes—although you've never had discussion about coffin preference. You were too busy living to be concerned with such details. Then you get word from the hospital that your loved one has survived. As he or she is wheelchaired down the main corridor, you weep gallons as your arms snake around the beloved's shoulders. Lazarus has returned.

A buddy's father had spent the last six months of his life in a nursing home. In his weakened state he continued to parent the way he did throughout my friend's life. He belittled him. He told him that he'd never be someone any father could be proud of. My friend graduated from Harvard, and held a responsible job. He was a therapist. His father told him his vocation was for 'weaklings'. "That's not a man's job", he told his son. Well, Dad contracted Covid-19 in the nursing home, and he changed. Radically. He asked his son for forgiveness. He noted how proud he was of the man his child had become, someone who used his skill to help others. Over the phone my friend noted that his atheism had turned to agnosticism. He said that at one point he lifted his eyes skyward, and said, "Thank you, Whoever you are."

There are other times in our lives when Christ goes AWOL, or so it seems. With this disease loved ones die quickly without opportunity for families to say good-bye. Sometimes Covid-19 upends special events on exact dates, the dagger's tip of Murphy's Law. A spouse dies the day before his or her retirement. A prospective husband or wife dies the evening before the wedding. The honoree for some special civic award misses opening remarks as she is rushed to the ER. 'Perfect timing' is euphemistic for divine malevolence. And in the light of this epidemic a vanishing Christ seems the last thing we need. 'Draw close to us,' we pray, 'and remove thoughts of coronavirus.' Recently I phoned an elderly parishioner, who is a shut-in. She sought my advice about a long standing problem. 'I prayed about this, but prayer doesn't help,' she said. 'I think God, Jesus, and Holy Spirit are drinking Pina Coladas on a tropical island somewhere; He's not in this room.'

When you sit down to eat, you pray for Christ's presence to be with you—but you sense nothing, save the ache of full-bodied loneliness. In light of Jesus' perceived absence we read the rosiest self-help book on our bookshelf, and parrot positive affirmations, over and over, until our mind staggers beneath the treacly weight our rational self can no longer buy. We sense we are in trouble when the sunny pronouncements of well-coiffed televangelists fall on deaf ears, our minds focusing instead on the sleek Italian suits they wear.

Let me repeat: Suppose Christ's presence and absence are poles which complement one another, and that the dialectic itself produces spiritual growth? Remember Jesus comes to the two disciples as a stranger, unrecognizable, yet he is near to them. Even when Christ seems absent, he still walks alongside us throughout our lives. But there is purpose for his seeming absence. If Christ were always recognizable, we'd take him for granted. The great medieval theologian, Meister Eckhart (1260–1327), noted that we'd treat an easily accessible deity the way we'd treat a cow; we'd take the milk and forget the bovine dispenser! I'm not at all sure the Almighty appreciated Eckhart's allusion! But the medieval Dominican has a point. It seems that in our pre-Covid-19 world, it is easy to believe faith is an entitlement, requiring no effort on our part.

"Work out your salvation with fear and trembling", Paul writes (Philippians 2:12). The Apostle is very aware that God still operates within us, but the Almighty's seeming absence calls us to apply personal effort, and risk. In Soren Kierkegaard's famous phrase, we must take the 'leap of faith', even when safety nets appear missing. Thus God's nature allows space for human struggle, and even a wrestling with the divine, as Jacob once did throughout one strange, numinous night (Genesis 32:22-32). Jesus states, "Seek and you will find" (Matthew 7:7). Often people believe seeking is too irksome. Not only would faith slacken, however. Too much security can smother us, can negate our ability to be the courageous men and women God calls us to be.

The early life of Gautama, the founder of Buddhism, illustrates this point. He was raised as a prince in a princely family. His parents made sure he never experienced the grittier aspects of human existence. In his twenties he grew restive, believing that there had to be more to life than the overprotection royalty provided. He escaped the castle, and walked the city streets, encountering what he had never seen: An old man, a sick man, and a dead man. With this new found understanding, he would finally develop his Middle Path.

Too little of God's presence and we topple into a rabbit hole of despair . Life becomes intolerable. The most eloquent and wrenching words ever written, I believe, about hopelessness came from the fifth century B.C.E. Greek tragedian, Sophocles. He wrote: "We are to the gods as flies are to wanton boys on a summer's day. They kill us for sport." We don't want to go there. Christ doesn't want us to go there. The good news is that even with a smidge of faith, Christ will maintain the delicate balance, the divine dialectic a growing belief system needs. God will neither allow you to slip into complacency, nor slide into nihilism. His way ,too, is the Middle Path.

PRAYER:

Lord, help me to understand that you are working your purpose in my life even when you seem distant. Work within me in your unique way so that I may exhibit the strength and courage of your son, Jesus. Let my words of encouragement, and my loving presence help those who, for a moment, experience your absence. Amen.

48

> "(Jesus said), 'If anyone will not welcome you, or listen to your words, shake off the dust from your feet as you leave that house or town'" Matthew 10:14.

> "But the populace incited the devout women of high standing, and the leading men of the city, and stirred up persecution against Paul and Barnabas, and drove them out of their region. So they shook the dust off their feet in protest against them, and went to Iconium. And the disciples were filled with joy and with the Holy Spirit" Acts 13:50-52.

> "Then Peter came and said to Jesus, 'Lord if another member of the church sins against me, how often should I forgive? As many as seven times?' Jesus said to him, 'Not seven times, but I tell you seventy-seven times.'" Luke 18:22-23.

> "Therefore as God's chosen people, holy and dearly loved, clothe yourselves with compassion, kindness, humility, gentleness and patience. Bear with each other and forgive one another as the Lord forgave you. And over all these virtues put on love which binds them altogether in perfect unity" Colossians 3:12-14.

Forgiveness is difficult. Covid-19 compounds. A friend tells you that he or she will call. You need not feel isolated; you'll never be alone. Distance can't separate the bond you share. Blah, blah. The call never comes. Multiply the 'fair weather friend' factor by two or three, and you feel as if you've 'fallen through the cracks', that if coronavirus seized you tomorrow, no one would ever know—or care. A long standing feud with a neighbor escalates because you and that person have quarantine time to nurse past slights. What about politicians who finesse insider trading, while a friend's home forecloses? Should they be forgiven? Let's shoot them instead! The constant threat of dying from Covid-19 shrinks our forgiveness store. So when Jesus counsels forgiveness 77 times, it seems beyond our capacity.

Paul's letter to the church at Colossae implies that bearing with one another, and forgiving one another are linked. In other words, forgiveness may take time. It may be a process, lifelong in some instances, rather than a knee-jerk response. Can we fulfill Jesus' command, while ignoring its emotional ramification? In her book, "Trauma and Recovery" psychiatrist Judith Herman suggests premature expressions of forgiveness can disempower. I believe she's correct. In pronouncing pardon head-wise, while denying heart throes, we bifurcate, we become doubleminded as the author of the book of James states (1:8). We self-condemn because we cannot follow wholeheartedly Christ's teaching.

Let's give ourselves a break. The Lord understands. He allows emotion to evolve. In the fallow time which coronavirus may provide, let's remember how God has forgiven us, time and again. That helps if we can maintain that focus. But often we can't, and the sentiment rings facile and pious. We may know God absolves, but the idea may not be enough to mitigate downright malice for someone who has hurt us deeply. I like Paul here. The great apostle follows Jesus in shaking off the dust against those who will not accept his message. We need not get angry at those who have wronged us. But we can move on, can't we? Perhaps we need to define pardon as 'giddyap' time.

The hardest people to forgive are those who feel they've done us no wrong. At a point in Jesus' ministry he tells his disciples that some may believe they're doing God a favor by hurting them. So we shake off the dust of our feet at the irreconcilables, those who would spurn our forgiveness if it were offered. Then we travel in God's hopeful direction, leaving their misdeeds in the rearview mirror. We try to forget. Even if we can't fully, we can still press forward. Notice, too, in Paul's case, joy follows dust shaking when he meets believers in a new city. God will provide new friends to fill the vacuum of those we leave behind.

Moving on is not easy. Sometimes it involves a symbolic act like shaking off the dust of our feet. I worked in Manhattan as an outpatient substance abuse clinician for four years. One of my clients had married a heroin user. Because she loved him, she became one too. Their ten year relationship ended when he overdosed. In order to preserve their love, she continued to inject. In group work, awareness dawned that her marriage was one of convenience—his. She had been manipulated and abused throughout.

As knowledge grew, she freed herself gradually from addiction. One day she visited her husband's ashes in a columbarium located in a nearby church. She placed a letter in the niche. It read, "Dearest. This is the last time I'll visit. I'm tired of mourning a relationship which nearly destroyed me. We're through. I'm getting on fine without you, and our mutual 'friend'. Maybe heroin was the only thing we had in common. It probably was. Good luck wherever you are. Good-bye." She read a copy to the support group. Interestingly four of the eight that evening also expressed the need to move away from destructive relationships.

What about you? Do you need to shake the dust off your feet to move forward? If so, have faith that our loving Lord is behind the insight, and will provide the very strength.

PRAYER:

> Lord, release my grudge holding ways. They mire me
> in the past, and contaminate my present. Help me to
> leave behind what is unhelpful and hurtful. Give me
> a hopeful vision of the future you indeed will grant.
> Amen.

PENTECOST

49

SCRIPTURE:

"'In the last days it will be, God declares, that I will
pour out my Spirit upon all flesh
And your sons and daughters will prophesy and your
young men shall see visions
And your old men shall dream dreams'"
Acts 2:17.

HIGH CAMP, HUAYNA POTOSI, BOLIVIA
16,300' April 26, 2003

Altitude increases coughing. High Camp rises thousands of feet above our base in the Condoriri Valley. Midnight. Hours earlier I wedged myself into a sleeping bag with everything I'll wear on the summit bid. The wind is steady and cold. Frost tendrils monogram the tent. Outer flaps snap dully in the wind imitating animal rustling. Neither the tent nor the sleeping bag retains body heat. Encased in wool and liner socks, my feet are ice blocks

I've been hacking for six hours, since we turned in at 6:00 p.m. A rasp has turned into a pleural ache which outlines my chest cavity. No stabs shortening deep breath. That's good. For now I'm pneumonia free, I think. In the last hour, however, a phlegmy rattle has replaced bronchial dryness. I examine my spit beneath the dim saffron colored beam of my miner's light. Red flecks indicate hemorrhage, the start of pulmonary edema. It looks okay, although I really can't tell. I'd rather not know. The thought of climbing Huayna Potosi with this life threatening problem seems easier than trying to explain the condition to my guide.

My Bolivian colleague, Vincentio, speaks no English. I return the favor by my inability to express even a smattering of Spanish.

We communicate well through pantomime: Thumbs up, belly rubbing for hunger, and caricature yawns signaling bed time. We've been climbing lesser peaks for two weeks now. It may be one of the best relationships I've ever had. Who needs language? If he were a woman I might drop to my knees and propose marriage!

We perch on a large stony outcrop. We hiked hours from our base camp. The narrow path often disappeared among slanting piles of rubble: Oblong slate slabs, and granite shards seamed with moss, and spotted with orange, amoeba shaped lichen. Below to our right and left, gashed, crenelated glaciers extend claws into the gray alluvium of disintegrating rock. The glacier veneer is soot colored and uniform as if a god has ironed dirt in place. Above, condors raft on lateral currents.

"Roberto", Vincentio calls, then rubs his stomach. Time for breakfast. He calls my name again. Instead of sleep I have spent time in various sleep positions. I shed my down-filled chrysalis, and cram numb feet into plastic boots. Gaiters strapped, I bend low and crab walk out the tent, leaving a cloud of air at the entrance. The massive luminescent flank of Huayna Potosi angles over me. Its chalky phosphorescence nibbles away at the darkness. Snowflakes flit before my headlamp. I tread carefully over arrowhead shaped slabs of talus, protruding at odd angles.

A dented fire-blackened metal tea pot sets on a flat stone, alongside plastic mugs, and packets of tea and instant oatmeal. I sprinkle coca leaves into a steaming cup of water. Vincentio does one better. He wedges several green coca leaves between his gum and cheek. Then, with a finger pinch, he combines it with white powder. He's leaching the drug from the leaf. He will climb the mountain in record pace. He stares at me glumly. He cares, but I did explain early on that I was a minister, by crossing myself repeatedly until he got the message. The information may not have pleased. I understand why. Centuries earlier his people were enslaved by the Spanish Conquistadors. One of the richest cities, Potosi, was built on the backs of indigenous people, Vincentio's ancestors, who worked the silver mines day and night until they keeled over and died. They were paid in coca leaves, so they'd labor longer and harder. Potosi boasted some of the most beautiful churches in the New World. Priests were not his people's protectors. I wonder if Vincentio resents me, or at least my vocation. Suspicion passes. He has become a dear friend in a short period of time.

I force down two cups because the tea prevents altitude sickness. It is followed by oatmeal, and a spotted, knapsack mashed banana. After breakfast, we descend the steep talus slope and arrive at the glacier where we strap crampons to boots. Crampons outline the boot sole, and have spikes which prevent slipping and sliding on snow and ice. The climb proper begins. Huayna Potosi lies near the equator which means one must summit before sunlight deconsolidates snow. Mountaineers die because of avalanches. I ascended a lower peak a week earlier in honor of a friend, a skilled mountaineer, who led a slow moving client to the summit. They got a late start. On the descent my friend was avalanched by afternoon heat. Fortunately his client survived. The ideal is to reach the peak at dawn or before, so most expeditions start around midnight.

We begin. As the slope steepens, we employ the French crampon method. One leg crosses the other like a speed skater on a turn. We trudge upward. My haunches ache. I begin to gobble the oxygen thinning air. I breathe deeply, hold, then exhale with a sigh. I was fine summiting four peaks over 17,000' feet several days ago. And I have climbed over 19,000' twice. This mountain rises slightly above 20,000'. I've topped out once at this height already. But this morning I can't catch my breath. We encounter a nearly vertical pitch. Vincentio works above me. I hear the tinkling of wine glasses as Vincentio repeatedly swings the tip of his ax into the ice. We are both held in place by dual crampon teeth extending from boot tips. Ice chips from Vincentio's effort cascade and echo off my helmet. I pick my way upward, following his lead. We are roped together, more for my safety than his. My calves cramp as they balance above the triangular crampon points.

We negotiate the ice wall, and stand before a large snowfield scored with crevasses. "We stop," Vincentio orders. Spires surround us, a few are topped with mortarboard slabs of snow. In the distance the lights of LaPaz burn ember orange. Lesser peaks in the

Cordillera Real loom darkly. I notice that the front lip of my wind parka has stiffened, breath's condensation. I remove my gloves and rummage in my summit-sack for water and a candy bar. After a few chews, I heave. Is the game up? Nausea is an early sign of altitude sickness. Then I start to cough. A sign of pulmonary edema. I dismiss the latter because I've been a 'cougher' since I was a little. That should have been my middle name.

"Ok?" Vincentio asks. He brushes his blue Gortex parka free of seam embedded ice.

"Am I?", I rasp. "Should we go back?" Vincentio cocks his head like a dog. Then he flashes 'thumbs-up' and grins. I guess that's the answer, although he may not have understood the question. I think he's simply a terrific optimist, and believes I can ascend with or without lungs. He won't let me surrender.

We toil up a 60 degree slope, moving in an S pattern to mitigate the pitch. I practice the stork step. March upward, and let the back leg bend while the knee-locked front leg carries the weight. Breathe deeply and start the process again. Stars dapple the sky, casting violet light on the snow. I focus on the headlamp illuminated snow six feet in front of me. I began the journey as a stargazer. Now neck muscles protest; craning consumes energy. On Huayna Potosi, my neck aligns with the imminent rather than the infinite. "Thin air theology," I think. Christianity calls the believer to resist temptation. Mountain theology calls one to resist tension.

Before I arrived in La Paz, I read the history of Bolivia. Huayna Potosi was sacred to the Tiwanaku, an ancient civilization which lasted nearly 3000 years. The Tiwanaku provided the cultural base for Incan successors, and their brief reign. The sun god of the Tiwanaku sported on this mountain, and ruled the seasons from its heights. Known as Viracocha to the Incas, it is sculpted, and pictured as a square headed deity with a huge flattened nose dominating the face. Sun rays stream from its head. Rectangular strips descend from the eyes, giving the cheeks a key-hole appearance. The strips represent tears. Some scholars suggest that the image is not of the god but of the priest who sacrificed to Viracocha. The priest cries because of his culture's unraveling sometime after 1000 AD. Either way, Huayna Potosi may pervade with the sadness of Vincentio's broken ancestors.

A sharp cracking bursts, as if a great tree has fallen. A muffled rumble. "Avalanche", I think. Somewhere above me snow descends at frightening speed. Vincentio and I stand before the steep 1000' summit pyramid. Above us head-lamps from two expeditions ornament the wall. Light beams skew across the sheer ice which has ripened to an inky blue in pre-dawn. Each rope linked party has the random form of loose thread on a dark jacket.

We start climbing the summit wall. Vincentio is 10 yards in front, working his ice ax with the rounded, economic gestures of a spider. The rope tugs against my climbing harness belted through my legs, and cinched at my waist by a primary harness, as wide and thick as a razor strop. I must keep up with my summit driven guide. He arches his back, providing greater leverage for his ax swing. Its point spears the ice, producing spray. I Inch upward on the front crampon teeth. Left boot, right boot, ax plant. Left boot, right boot, ax plant. There's the Texas Two-Step, and the Mountaineering Two-Step. One is a dance of life. Cold sprints through my body. Are my lungs disintegrating? Oxygen speeds through with no affects. Vincentio tugs the rope; I don't move, although I assume I have. Plant the ice ax, and move your boots, the mind commands. "The flesh is willing but the spirit is...whatever it is." Is that how Jesus' saying goes? Probably not.

I'm nearly on top. I rest my head on the ice wall and squint. The wall pulses cold. My head, flywheel heavy, rotates to the east, engaging the horizon. Slats of light, the iridescent blue of a peacock's neck, peek through the jalousie of waning night. Vincentio tugs the rope again. Calf muscles spasm. It's hard to respond. The scrape of my crampons seems a faint echo. Then it happens. I peel off the wall backwards, my arms wind milling. The nylon rope arrests my fall suddenly. The harness bites into my back, and I snap upright and perpendicular, once again, to the snow field below. The rope's elasticity overcompensates. It tightens, then launches like a slingshot, slamming me nose first against the ice wall. I droop like a discarded marionette. My teeth chatter. Somehow my ice ax has punctured my cheek. Soon I swallow the metallic taste of my blood. Red splotches appear on my parka when I exhale. My nose may be broken.

Movement skitters above me. Suddenly Vincentio lands beside, bobbing from the pliancy of a second rope. I smell licorice and coca on his breath. Gloves removed, he fastens a second rope to the front of my climbing harness. I hear the metallic carabiner snap. Vincentio leaves as suddenly as he arrived. Soon he and another guide are hoisting me to the summit.

On top the two guides chatter in the clipped tones of Aymara, their native language, as they rub my hands. Vincentio offers pills which I swallow. I hope they contain cocaine. "You okay?" the second guide asks as he helps me re-glove. "Okay now?" The guide is beefier than Vincentio. His front teeth are bracketed with silver. "Do you know about the silver mines of Potosi?" I ask him as Vincentio kneels patting my back as I reel off coughs.

"Potosi was very rich. The conquistadores enslaved your people, and forced them to work in the silver mines of Cerro Rico." The second guide knows more English than Vincentio. He laughs. "Tourist traps, maybe?" He laughs. Vincentio joins him. "How you say?" Vincentio asks his friend. "Tourist traps", he repeats. They both laugh. So much for history.

By this time Vincentio gazes toward La Paz. "See, Roberto. See". Exhaustion furls. I gaze at the nearest section, and spot the lights of the airport, some blinking, their poles thin, turning diaphanous like icicles, in dawn's light. The LaPaz airport is one of the highest in the world. Landing above 12,000', one can become hypoxic or unconscious when he or she exits. Acclimatizing begins on the tarmac, the joke goes.

"See, Roberto", Vincentio repeats. "See". The layered cloud banks hovering above the city begin to fade. Purple and pink ribbons levitate horizontally with the stateliness of ocean liners. Beneath them the rounded hills glow with grass. Cars are spotted coming and going in the heart of the city. From our vantage, they meld like mercury streaming.

After Huayna Potosi, and before our final climb, Vincentio takes me to his small apartment in a neighborhood near the airport. The walls were whitewashed, maybe a decade earlier, so they are patterned with smudge. There is a photo of Huayna Potosi, roughly cut from a magazine, and mounted in a dime store frame. On the other wall, a photo of the Virgin of Guadalupe, also scissored out, and tacked without a frame.

The apartment has one bedroom. Vincentio sleeps on the couch. The bedroom belonged to his mother. There is a black and white photo of her, and Vincentio as a child, taken, it seems, from a photograph booth at a carnival. The boy's head rests on his mother's shawled chest, and they are caught in a blink, giggling. They are innocents in front of the camera. The photograph rests against his mother's pillow. A large stool next to the bed serves as a nightstand. On it is a wooden cross, and three or four votive candles. I'm unsure when she died, and don't ask. Vincentio has a six pack of ginger ale, and little else in his refrigerator. He offers me a can, and I accept. We click our cans as a toast. One more mountain to climb. This one is higher than Huayna Potosi, but I can tell by his enthusiastic thumbs-up that I will make it. And I do. For him ginger ale is costly. I have a hunch that the outfitter who employs him is his main food source. For me, in this moment, the soda becomes sacramental.

A Formica topped kitchen table sits in the middle of the room, the kind my parents owned when I was a child in the 1950's. On it is a photo of the mighty Himalayan peak, Dhaulagiri. Someday Vincentio hopes to climb it. Its south face is arguably the hardest big wall in the world. He believes he's up for the challenge. If he can lug me to the summit of Huayna Potosi, well then Dhaulagiri will be a piece of cake!

In April I dreamed about Vincentio, and our expedition 17 years earlier. I had thought of him since we said good-bye. I took photos. Several years later I wrote a short story in which he figures. Nonetheless neither he nor Huayna Potosi had ever entered my dreams, until the outbreak. The effect of Covid-19 is that a certain realism penetrates my subconscious. I know why. The coronavirus world seems surreal, a waking nightmare. Thus our sleep fantasies represent pre-epidemic realities, providing a counterbalance to the incomprehensible daily dreamscape.

Nevertheless sleep's distortion arrived at the summit. Near base camp there is a little cemetery where the names of dead climbers are inscribed on slate shards. Such roughhewn plots exist beside many high peaks. There a sound emanates. As Vincentio, his friend and I gaze in the distance at LaPaz' reawakening, the air stirs behind us. Suddenly the blare of a thousand bugles shakes the summit; our climbing helmets spin free, our hair roaches. The sound morphs into an unalloyed stream of wailing. No words. The thrumming intensifies and sharpens into howling.

I awake. And understand. What mountain would be more relevant for this numinous event than the home of a weeping deity. The howling implores the living to absorb their unfinished hopes and dreams as we move forward. 'Don't forget us', they lament. 'If you do, the virus has won.' We won't. We will complete, in some way, paths cut short by the virus. There's mutuality here. The author of Hebrews notes that a great cloud of witnesses in heaven watch us as we run our races of faith (12:1). May we do so in their honor, confident that their encouragement will provide the strength and grit to ascend Covid-19.

Huayna Potosi was the mountain which came closest to ending my life. Apart from exhaustion, I've never had trouble on other peaks. And Vincentio winched me to the summit for a pittance. I compensated him well after the climb because I understood that the local outfitter probably wouldn't. Let Vincentio represent all of the deplorably paid workers in our country today who risk themselves on a variety of front lines, so that folks like us might be safe. We are roped to them, and they are our lifelines when we fall. God bless them, and their daily Christ-like sacrifices.

Let Vincentio also represent people of color in our society who are most susceptible to this scourge, and the terrible inequities which consign impoverished minorities to the highest risk category. Jesus said, "Blessed are you who are poor, for yours is the kingdom of God" (Luke 6:20). Vincentio embodies Jesus' words. In his cramped apartment with little more than memory of his mother, and mountaineering hopes which most likely were dashed by indigence, he exhibited a generosity and unconquerable spirit which could save the world if it were bottled.

Then there is the mountain itself. Huayna Potosi. Today we climb a terrible peak, Covid-19, and it will take all of us, roped together, to attain the final victory, which indeed we will. But climbing involves suffering. There is no easy ascent. Let us accept affliction as part of the upward journey. It cannot be avoided. Let us ascend bearing the crosses of others as well our own. When we fall, may we be assured that God will leap from the summit, and lift us upward, or send human rescuers to accomplish His will. And when we reach the top, may we gaze at the dawn of a post coronavirus world, shorn of selfishness and division.

Finally there's my cough. I certainly hacked my way up the mountain. But I had done so in any number of athletic pursuits throughout my life. Wrestling, boxing, swimming, heck, even a spirited game of ping pong jump-started the reflex. Several years after Huayna Potosi, I was diagnosed with a genetic blood clotting disorder. Sometime later in my life—the hematologist has no clue when—, it combined with a non-genetic blood clotting disorder. I bet they're best friends! I have since become the pharmaceutical companies' gold star client for blood thinning medication. I cough little now. There are no more mountains in my future because I need to be relatively near a hospital if I cut myself. Instead of a cougher I've become a bleeder. And I have other lung issues beside which elicits the macabre hope that one day my unique pair will be displayed at the Smithsonian or perhaps a "Ripley's Believe It Or Not" museum. This book may not sell a stitch, but my lungs may be the ticket to post-mortem recognition.

Not that my diagnoses have hindered me much. In 2016, at age 68, I crossed the country on a bicycle, from San Francisco to Portsmouth New Hampshire, averaging 82 miles a day. The greatest miracle in my life however is this: For 61 years I had no idea I was a clotting factory. None. I should have been crowned 'Rev. Pulmonary Edema in Waiting' early on. I should be dead by now. No physician diagnosed the problem until Dr. Doug when I returned to the mid-Hudson valley. Let me repeat: I should have died years ago. But I didn't. Obviously. Which means that when God wants me, He'll let me know. And, by the way, He'll let you know too. Until that time let us live each day fully, and freely knowing that the One who loves us, and holds us in the palm of his hand will orchestrate our comings and goings. Let's leave our dying fears to God. That's where they belong. Believe that you are loved, inestimably, by the One who created you in His image. And live with joy and hope in the present, this day, every day.

PRAYER:

> Lord, let me undertake the challenges set before me. Let me climb spiritual Everests, bringing others along. May we sight a future promised land free from epidemic. Let us polish our dancing shoes in anticipation for the celebration which will occur with Covid-19's defeat. Thank you for your abiding presence throughout this journey. I love you, Lord, more than words can express. Amen.

June 10, 2020.

CPSIA information can be obtained
at www.ICGtesting.com
Printed in the USA
BVHW030830281220
596556BV00007B/96